More Tales from the Cubs Dugout

Bob Logan

Sports Publishing L.L.C.
www.sportspublishingllc.com

Director of production: Susan M. Moyer
Project manager: Jim Henehan
Dust jacket design: Kerri Baker
Developmental editor: Mark Zulauf
Copy editor: Cindy McNew

ISBN: 1-58261-561-6

Printed in the United States of America

Sports Publishing L.L.C.
www.sportspublishingllc.com

Contents

Foreword

(Author's note: the No. 26 flag atop Wrigley Field's right field foul pole teaches new generations of Cubs fans that Billy Williams was—and is—part of Chicago sports history. Nobody has worn a Cubs uniform longer than he—16 years as a player, 15 as a coach. And few hitters have provided more pleasure for Cubs fans than No. 26, the Sweet Swinger, piling up 2,510 hits, 392 homers and 1,353 RBIs. Now in his third North Side career as an aide to Cubs president Andy MacPhail, Williams adds the same character and class he displayed on the field.)

When I came to Chicago in 1959, there were a lot of empty seats in Wrigley Field, because the Cubs weren't winning. All that changed when Leo Durocher took over as our manager (1966), and since then, the excitement among our fans has been growing, year by year. With Dusty Baker coming aboard to manage the Cubs, I have a new role, working with the young outfielders and doing whatever I can to help Andy and Ted [Hendry] get the Cubs to where we all want to go—the World Series.

The one thing that's never changed for all these years in Wrigley Field has been the fans. Cubs fans are unbelievable. They never give up, sticking with us through some tough times and bitter disappointments. My biggest regret in baseball is not bringing the World Series to Chicago in 1969, after the Cubs lit up the whole town all summer. I still believe we had the best team in baseball that year, but we just couldn't get it done.

Another thing I grew to enjoy was the way the veteran Chicago sportswriters did their jobs. I wasn't much of a talker when I first got to the Cubs, but they were fair and honest about the way I played the game. Writers like Ed Prell, Jim Enright, Jerome Holtzman, and Bob Logan had a lot to do with the fans' support for me. I want a World Series ring for myself, but I want it even more for those fans.

Billy Williams

Preface

The easiest part of writing this book was deciding on the dedication.

When it comes to being dedicated, nobody can outfinish Cub fans. That's all the more amazing, because the Cubs have been outfinished by almost everybody in baseball since I started covering them in 1970. Now into my fourth decade as a Cubwatcher, I've run the gamut of emotions with this flummoxed franchise and many of the lummoxes wandering around Wrigley Field in their uniform.

Through it all, the lone hard core of Cubs consistency has been these indescribable, indomitable fans. I've seen them roasting in the summer sun, shivering under blankets through the raw winds of April and chilling fog that blots out the scoreboard in September, roaring—and pouring—while torrents of rain pour into the bleachers.

Ah, those Wrigley bleachers. Lots more about them in chapter 3 of this book, the fans' own turn at bat. But for all of you, in or out of the bleachers, you've earned my admiration and respect. Cubs fans everywhere, this book's for you.

I am grateful to John McDonough, the Cubs' outstanding marketing and broadcasting chief, for his friendship and assistance over the years. Also, many thanks to Cubs publicists Blake Cullen, Chuck Shriver, Bob Ibach, Ned Colletti, Sharon Pannozzo, Chuck Wasserstrom and Samantha Newby for their able assistance.

Bob Logan

CHAPTER 1

THE LAST QUOTER

The Chicago Cubs have walked the walk into the postseason promised land just three times since 1945, when they lost their last World Series.

But in the fifty-plus futile seasons their fans endured during baseball's longest famine, aside from the flickering feasts of 1984, 1989 and 1998, the Cubs still talked the talk. Oh, brother, as Jack Brickhouse used to say, did they ever!

So there's no better way for Cubs junkies to get a daily fix of Wrigley Field fever—and fervor—than by talking about their beloved bunglers. Or by listening to the Cubs talk about themselves, rehashing and reliving every agonizing minute of this frantic trip through good times (few) and bad (as usual) for the Little Team that Very Seldom Could.

Lots more than half the fun in all those frustrating summers is the endless array of might-have-been, should-have-been, could-have-been and why-not theories, fantasies, alibis and arguments over the plight of our loveable losers. My bulging file of Cubs quotes, almost as entertaining as sun-deviled Cubs infielders in pursuit of a windblown Wrigley popup, provides plenty of insight but few solutions.

Understandably, this baffling mystery has spread from a hallowed patch of turf on Chicago's North Side to Cubs diehards across the country and around the world. What keeps killing the Cubs? Here are a few hundred suspects.

Lessons from Leo

Few managers in baseball history stirred up more conflicting emotions than Leo Durocher. During his stormy sojourn (1966-72) as fiery field boss of the Cubs, Leo the Lip aroused adulation bordering on worship among fans and fury that sometimes boiled over in the clubhouse. His shouting matches with such emotional players as Ron Santo and Joe Pepitone, among others, came perilously close to mayhem at times.

Even the nicest of Cub nice guys, Ernie Banks, drew his share of scorn from the manager, who was credited as declaring (although he actually didn't), "Nice guys finish last." So did shortstop Don Kessinger, a genial Southerner who survived the Durocher era to go down as one of the all-time top Cubs at his position.

"When Leo came to Chicago, the first thing I heard him say was, 'We've got to find a shortstop,'" Kessinger recalled. "He said I couldn't hit, field or throw."

A sensitive man, Kessinger at times was nearly in tears, because he took to heart some Durocher tirades that most veteran players merely shrugged off. Although he disliked

Leo's methods, Kessinger soaked up lots of baseball acumen from the brash manager, who broke in during the Roaring Twenties with the legendary Bronx Bombers—the Yankees of Babe Ruth. When Kessinger took over as manager of the White Sox in 1979, the mild-mannered skipper remembered what he had learned from the crusty baseball icon.

"When I made a move, I used to stop and think, 'Hey, I learned that from Leo,'" Kessinger recalled.

Brian, Can You Pitch?

B rian Urlacher flashed his speed in Wrigley Field before the Bears' top 2000 draft pick made his first NFL tackle. As soon as he got tapped to play in Soldier Field, the All-American linebacker from New Mexico U. hot-footed it to the North Side to throw out the first pitch before the Cubs lost to the Florida Marlins on April 16, 2000.

"I grew up rooting for the Cubs, and seeing a game in this park is a dream come true," said Urlacher, a New Mexico native. "Shane Andrews [another of the 80 or so pretenders who've had a cup of coffee at third base for the Cubs since Ron Santo departed in 1974] is still an idol at home."

'69 on Our Minds

T he September swoon of the 1969 Cubs is the stuff of legend, still sticking in their faithful fans' craws more than three decades later. It sent shockwaves through

Ernie Banks, flanked by his wife and another Hall of Famer, Hoyt Wilhelm, shakes off the disappointment of 1970 with a cheerful prediction for '71. It didn't happen, but that never deters Mr. Cub from issuing the same rosy forecast every year.

Chicago, especially on the North Side, where Wrigleyville went into virtual mourning.

There were worse disappointments to come, especially in 1984, when the Cubs finally snapped the Billy Goat jinx that had kept them out of postseason action since 1945. Weeks, even months later, a joyous banner still hung above the entrance to the firehouse at Waveland Street and Sheffield Avenue, across the street from Wrigley Field: "Official Firehouse of the 1984 World Series."

It was not to be, because the Cubs staged a colossal collapse in San Diego, falling one game short of their goal after storming to a 2-0 lead in the best-of-five series. The oh-so-close firehouse banner swayed sadly in the winter wind swirling through the deserted ballpark, a harbinger of even quicker Cubs playoff exits in 1989 and '98.

Selma the Savior

O ver the years, millions of words and billions of Cubs fan laments keep postmortem-ing and second-guessing those foldups. In seeking to sort it all out and explain the inexplicable, they always come back to the same plaintive wail: "Why? Why? Why?"

Cubs fans know they might as well try to turn the Hawk—the icy blast off the Lakefront that transports Chicago to a February suburb of Siberia—into a balmy breeze as to explain the unfathomable. Amid the pile of hand-wringing lamentations, this conversation with quirky ex-Cubs pitcher Dick Selma, from his home in Mexico, emerged as my favorite memory of 1969, that sensational summer that made the fatal fall hurt much more.

Free-spirited reliever Selma appointed himself the official cheerleader of the left field Bleacher Bums in 1969. His towel-waving antics began one day when the Cubs fell behind in Wrigley Field. Selma yelled to the bleacher creatures from his bullpen perch, "It isn't over yet. Make some noise!"

The Bums erupted, Ernie Banks homered, and the Cubs won. From that moment on, superstitious Cubs manager Leo Durocher barked orders to "Get 'em stirred up!" Selma gleefully obliged, and a Cubs tradition was born, overflowing into a season-long jubilee of songs, cheers, chants and zany

antics by the Bleacher Bums, adorned with yellow hard hats
and led by bullhorn-wielding Ron Grousl.

"When Leo saw what I was doing and how the Bums
reacted, he told me to keep doing it every day," Selma
recalled. "Despite how things turned out, the way those fans
lived and died with us made that one of the best times in
my life."

After the ecstasy turned to agony, trampled under a 41-
12 closing stampede by the New York Mets, Selma departed
with fond memories of the National League pennant that
got snatched away. They include the following excerpt from
a letter written to him by a Bleacher Bum's mother:

"You kept my son off the street and in the bleachers.
His hero is Billy Williams, instead of Fidel Castro. Ron
Santo's autograph is worth more to him than a stolen hubcap.
And how can an LSD trip beat a trip to Wrigley Field?"

Kerry Wood, but Cubs Wouldn't

The fallout from more than a half-century of
franchise failures still haunts competitors like
combative Cubs pitcher Kerry Wood. The fireballing right-
hander fought back from a career-threatening injury,
submitting to Tommy John elbow surgery on April 8, 1999,
and missing that entire season to recuperate.

But Wood's blend of overpowering stuff and will to win
couldn't prevent the Cubs from barging into the new
millennium with the same old results, losing 97 games in
2000, falling apart after making some early noise in 2001

and turning 2002 into total disaster. After a 3-0 loss in St. Louis on May 13 greased the skids for manager Don Baylor's firing, Wood's frustration boiled over in a profanity-laced postgame tirade.

"We're dead," Wood admitted angrily. "The Cubs are playing like we're already out of the [NL Central Division] race. I'm tired of this same old stuff about 'Keep your head up and we'll get 'em tomorrow.' It's not happening."

Things got even worse from there. When dependable starter Jon Lieber—the first Cub 20-game winner (20-6 in 2001) since Greg Maddux went 20-11 in 1992—departed with arm trouble, the inevitable result of too many elbow-straining sliders, the Cubs hit bottom. To those ever-hopeful fans, Wood's outrage brought back echoes of futility from the past.

Murcer Pleads for Mercy

B obby Murcer was supposed to out-Sammy Sosa in 1977, when the Cubs acquired the supposed slugger from San Francisco in a bad trade that shipped recalcitrant third baseman Bill Madlock to the Giants. Murcer arrived amid much fanfare from general manager Bob Kennedy and field boss Herman Franks. He contributed modest team-best totals of 27 homers and 89 RBIs in his debut, while the Cubs improved by six games that season, inching up to .500 at 81-81. They promptly sank again in '78, and Murcer went back to the Yankees, where he earlier had been touted as the next Mickey Mantle.

Murcer found handy scapegoats to explain his so-so performance—the rest of the Cubs and the San Francisco fog.

"When you're around dead people, you play like you are dead," Murcer moaned. "In Chicago, there was all that day ball. It was so cold and windy in San Francisco, you didn't like playing ball. Both places, I never felt I belonged."

Franks, not much of a humorist, got a laugh out of that complaint.

"I see where Murcer made a bad throw that cost the Yankees a game last night," the rotund Cubs manager said. "Funny he should talk about us now."

Phoney Excuse

Shortly before his roller-coaster tenure with the Cubs ended in 1972, manager Leo Durocher provided a painful glimpse inside the confusion that prevented his sagging squad from finding some fresh bodies. Calls to general manager John Holland from other teams seeking deals went unanswered shortly before the trading deadline. Holland was meeting with his embattled manager in Durocher's clubhouse office.

"If they'd put the calls down here on my line, we might have been able to make a trade," Leo the Lion mumbled, his roar muffled by almost seven years of inability to lead the Cubs into the playoffs.

But the communications gap within the Cubs organization went deeper than that. Leo had moved, without giving Holland his new phone number.

"I don't know any more than you do," Holland told frustrated sports scribes, scrambling to contact the elusive Durocher.

But the Billy Goat hex, slapped on the Cubs by Chicago character William Sianis when the Cubs refused to let his pet goat enter Wrigley Field with him for the 1945 World Series, apparently afflicted the front office as well as the team. Sianis's nephew, Sam, still runs the Billy Goat Inn, made famous on *Saturday Night Live* ("Chizborger! Chizborger!") as a hangout for such thirsty Chicago newspaper types as the legendary Mike Royko.

Mysteriously balky telephones also got general manager Jim Frey's goat while he was trying to beat the 1989 trade deadline.

"The phones went out for four hours, and I couldn't talk to anyone," Frey grumbled.

Lou Loses

A winner on the field and in the broadcast booth, former Cubs manager Lou Boudreau got caught with the team in the 1977 power blackout that turned off the lights in New York and much of the Eastern seaboard. Easy-going Lou found a way to make light of the situation, along with his own well-earned reputation as another of Chicago handicapper Dave Feldman's legion of "BDHs"— broken-down horseplayers.

"I lost all my money," Boudreau said of the peril lurking on New York's pitch-black streets. "But it was this afternoon, at the race track."

Meanwhile, Cubs catcher Steve Swisher confessed that he found somebody willing to spend the dark night with him.

"Unfortunately, it was a guy," Swisher said. "This is some city."

A Familiar Target

During his productive 19-year playing career with a half-dozen American League clubs, ex-Cubs manager Don Baylor grew used to wearing a bullseye on his uniform. Baylor chalked up the big-league record for getting hit by pitches a total of 267 times.

It hurt a lot more when Baylor became the chief target of criticism for the injury-riddled Cubs' foldup in 2002. As usual in such situations, the players survived, but the manager didn't. While he was struggling through his rocky 65-97 inaugural as Cubs field boss in 2000, Baylor lamented the way batters nowadays tend to charge the mound, triggering a brawl, when pitchers try to work inside.

"When I got hit you could even the score by taking out somebody on the other team with a hard slide," Baylor said. "Now you have to stay three feet away from fielders.

"Frank Robinson stood on top of the plate, and he got hit plenty. If pitchers are throwing at your head, it's just part of the game. I hope we don't turn into the NBA, where the coach has to keep his players on the bench when a fight starts."

That never was a problem for Leo Durocher, who often told his pitchers "Stick it in his ear," if an opposing hitter's bat got too hot. Even after he retired, Durocher watched

TV games with disdain when umpires warned pitchers not to throw too close to batters.

"I agree with Larry Goetz, a tough old umpire, about beanballs," Durocher said. "He told me he couldn't look inside a pitcher's head to tell whether he was throwing at anybody. He was right. The hitters have to protect themselves."

Ray Knows the Way

Ray Burris saw his share of losing under four different Cubs managers from 1973-79. They produced a .500 record just once in that span (81-81 in 1977), but Burris was their leading winner twice, with back-to-back 15-victory seasons in 1975-76.

So the veteran right-hander knew what Herman Franks was up against in 1981, when that ex-Cubs manager replaced Bob Kennedy as general manager. A straight shooter, right-hander Burris came into Wrigley Field with the Montreal Expos to sum up the situation.

"Maybe the Cubs are the worst team in baseball, but I hate to see what they're going through right now," Burris told me. "Does that mean the fans should go out and shoot them? Can the Cubs go down to Western Avenue and pick up 25 new players?

"Take a young pitcher in this park, where the ball jumps when the wind's blowing out. If he gets rocked in a few starts, the fans get on him, the media writes and talks like he's a dog and he gets no support from the front office. I know, because all that happened to me here."

Poison-to-Poison Call

Bob Rush was an effective Cubs pitcher from 1948 through 1957. Like all starters, though, he went to the Wrigley Field mound without good stuff one afternoon, and line drives soon began chopping shrubbery off the ivy-covered walls. Manager Phil Cavarretta stood it as long as he could before making a long, slow trip from the dugout, while the Cubs bullpen sprang into action.

"I have to take you out," he told Rush. "Our outfielders are getting poison ivy."

Going Backwards

Injuries left the Cubs in a jam throughout their season-long plummet in 2002, but it happens to them a lot. Even a traffic jam put catcher Joe Girardi in a jam during his first tour of duty with the Cubs. Already idled by back problems, Girardi got caught in typical postgame gridlock on Clark Street. While waiting for it to get unsnarled, he felt more back pain. Instead of going on the road with the team, Girardi had to stay home—and out of traffic.

Game of Real Life

Along with the rest of America, the Cubs paused on Sept. 11, 2002, to pay tribute to victims on the first anniversary of the terror attacks. And, like the rest of us, they faced the reality that such things can happen here.

"It would be very difficult to detect one person carrying something into a crowded ballpark," said pitcher Kerry Wood. "I'm not worried about myself, but I think everybody's concerned about their family and wondering how secure we are anywhere in the country."

Sammy Sosa, a native of the Dominican Republic, used his role as the team leader to speak out for America. He lifted the spirits of Cubs fans and TV viewers after homering on Sept. 27, 2001, the first Wrigley Field game since the terrorist attacks on New York and Washington, D.C.

"God wanted me to show my appreciation for America," Sosa said of the way he carried two small American flags, handed to him by first base coach Billy Williams, on his trip around the bases. "I did it out of respect for America, which means a lot to me."

Cosell vs. Caray

Howard Cosell, the biggest thing in sports broadcasting when he was the ringmaster for Frank Gifford, Dandy Don Meredith, and others on *Monday Night Football* telecasts, was no fan of Harry Caray.

"There is no excuse for Caray's cheerleading," Cosell fumed after watching Harry turn Comiskey Park into Carayland, USA during a televised White Sox game. "I was amazed when I heard him leading the fans in singing 'Take Me Out to the Ball Game.' Caray's broadcasts are on the grade-school level.

"It's true all sports announcers are housemen to an extent, but some more than others," Cosell continued, warming to his diatribe. "I once had high hopes for [former Chicago sportswriter and TV sportscaster] Brent Musberger. I thought he would be the next Howard Cosell, but he has become a high school cheerleader. He's not as bad as Harry Caray, though."

Fortunately for Cosell's massive ego, he was not asked to comment later on the way Caray wrapped Wrigley Field fans around his finger and became America's favorite cheerleader after moving to the Cubs' TV booth in 1982.

Quick Double Dip Trip

Seemingly endless games have become a problem in the major leagues, especially in Chicago. Although the White Sox seem to specialize in three and a half-hour marathons, the Cubs now take longer to totter through nine innings as well. It's hard to imagine that on Sept. 4, 1957, the Cubs not only followed Ernie Banks's favorite rallying cry—"Let's play two today"—but did so in double-quick fashion.

They reeled off the first Wrigley Field game against the Cincinnati Reds in a mere hour and 37 minutes before slowing somewhat through a two-hour, 20-minute nightcap. Still, the whole afternoon in the Friendly Confines took just three hours and 57 minutes.

Mayday? No, May Night

The Cubs' first-ever Wrigley Field night game was supposed to be on 8/8/88, but maybe the Billy Goat hex applied to arc lights as well as day games. Persistent rain forced the Cubs to call it off and try again against the Mets on Aug. 9. It rained on their parade again 10 years later, pushing that first pitch back to 9:17 p.m. on April 30, 1998, the latest-ever Wrigley Field starting time. The game didn't finish until the next month—at 12:15 a.m. on May 1.

Hooton No Historian

B urt Hooton didn't give a hoot about the possibility of equaling Johnny Vander Meer's feat—back-to-back no-hitters. The Cincinnati lefty did it in 1938 against the Boston Bees (later the Milwaukee/Atlanta Braves) on June 11 and the Brooklyn (now Los Angeles) Dodgers on June 15. Hooton, a 22-year-old Cub rookie, made the quantum leap from the University of Texas to the bigs by no-hitting the Phillies 4-0 in Wrigley Field on April 16, 1972.

The media crush in those days was nothing like the mob hounding players and jamming clubhouses after games now, especially with shoulder-mounted TV cameras. Even so, Hooton got grilled exhaustively after making the Phils knuckle under with his pet pitch, a dazzling knuckle curve. He was astonished that anyone would expect him to do it again in his next start, a Shea Stadium outing against the Mets.

"I never heard of Vander Meer," the exasperated Hooton said. "The reporters were looking at me like I was some kind of fool because I didn't know who he was. I'm not up on baseball history, and pitching two no-hitters in a row never crossed my mind."

Not to worry. Hooton did not twirl another no-no. The chunky right-hander went 10-14 for the Cubs in the rest of the 1972 season and failed to win consistently until he got traded to the Dodgers, three years later.

Mr. Consistency

Jon Lieber, Opening Day starter for the Cubs in 2001 and 2002, paid the price for his consistent brilliance. The Cubs declined to pick up his 2003 contract option, making the sturdy right-hander a free agent. The strain of working more than 200 innings for three straight years, including an NL-high 251 in 2000, finally took its toll on Lieber's pitching arm. He'll be missed, on the mound and in the clubhouse, while he tries to come back with the Yankees.

"My job is to take us into the seventh inning with a chance to win the game," the unassuming Lieber kept telling us after his typical no-nonsense starts. He got the ball and threw it, keeping the Cubs' defense alert and opposing runners off the bases with masterful control. Lieber went 20-6 in 2001, joining Greg Maddux (1992), Rick Sutcliffe (1984) and Rick Reuschel (1977) as the Cubs' only 20-game winners since Fergie Jenkins did it for six straight seasons. (1967-72).

Tuff Act to Follow

Opening Day at Wrigley Field is a blue-letter day in Chicago, as in Cubbie Blue. Maybe the most

Ferguson Jenkins (hands on hips) takes a detour en route to the Hall of Fame while the Cubs pitcher hears a lecture from umpire Chris Pelekoudas. Later in that same 1969 season, the Bleacher Bums got revenge on Pelekoudas by making him run all the way out to the left field wall.

spectacular moment was Willie Smith's two-run pinch homer in the 11th inning on April 8, 1969, giving the Cubs a 7-6 victory over the Phillies. That put Leo Durocher's confident club in first place, where they stayed for the next 155 days, touching off a matching wave of hysteria and an epidemic of pennant fever that spread from coast to coast, like a giant (not San Francisco Giant, of course) tsunami.

But for sheer power, not even Sammy Sosa could match the three-homer 1994 Opening Day outburst by unheralded Cubs center fielder Karl "Tuffy" Rhodes. He astonished the jam-packed Wrigley Field throng by starting the Cubs' first turn at bat with a homer off Mets ace Dwight Gooden. Warming to his task, he connected off Gooden in each of his next two trips.

"I've never seen somebody come out of the gate like that," said Cubs manager Tom Trebelhorn.

Neither had Cubs fans, joyously preparing to anoint lefty swinger Tuffy their new Teddy, as in Ted Williams. Alas, it didn't last, and neither could the lead provided by his trio of round-trippers. The Cubs lost that opener 12-8. Rhodes's magic bat faded soon after, like many of the baseball flowers that bloom in the spring, or until pitchers get loose when the weather warms.

As the old story goes, rookies begin calling home when cutdown date arrives at big-league training camps to voice the same plaintive wail: "Put another bean in the pot, Ma. The pitchers are starting to throw curves."

Rhodes wasn't a rookie, and he had a few more bright moments, notably a pair of homers against the Astros on April 28 at the Astrodome. But Tuffy batted a meek .201 from May 1 to the end of the 1994 season, collecting only 38 hits in 189 trips. Still, unlike many "can't-miss" hotshot Cubs prospects over the years, Rhodes had his big moment in the sun—actually, three of them in a row at that electrifying home opener.

CHAPTER 2

YOU CAN'T BEAT FUN GUYS AT THE OLD BALLPARK

O f all the endangered species in baseball, the certified screwball ranks right up there with the two-hour game, the $2 beer and the .200 hitter making less than $2 million per year. It's big business now, much too big for monkey business (except in Anaheim) or showbiz antics to intrude on the money machine that will rake in $3.7 *billion* for all 28 major-league clubs in 2003. That includes even the cash-strapped Puerto Rico Expos.

There are a few exceptions, notably Barry Bonds's leisurely saunter from the plate after rocketing one of his moonshots into McCovey Cove at Pac Bell Park. But neither that nor Sammy Sosa's trademark homer hip-hop is considered hot doggery, with or without mustard and relish. That's because (a) both are superstars, more gigantic than the Giants and more colossal than the Cubs, and (b) Early Wynn and Don Drysdale are dead. If those two combative right-handers were still around, Bonds and Sosa would be smart to wear a suit of armor on their next trip to the plate after homering off them.

Most baseball brawls nowadays erupt when a batter charges the mound in righteous wrath at a pitch that veers slightly off the inside corner. The game's etiquette and individual testosterone levels then demand that dozing bench players awaken and join the melee, along with bullpen exiles, reluctantly interrupting their national pastime—girl-watching in the stands. Somehow, I doubt that Harry Caray's ritual chant ("You Can't Beat Fun at the Old Ballpark") included these occasional rugby scrums.

But there always will be a place for another Dizzy Dean or Mark "The Bird" Fydrich, if clones of those delightful screwballs ever make it to the big leagues. Chances are their agents, lawyers, accountants and financial advisors will convince them that skylarking is bad business.

So I scrutinize rosters every spring, in a vain search for the next Jay Johnstone. This light-hearted goofball was fun to be around, pulling pranks to enliven every clubhouse and ballpark he entered. As a reward, Johnstone got abruptly released by the Cubs in 1984, because general manager Dallas Green, in grim pursuit of the Cubs' first postseason berth for 39 years, wasn't about to tolerate such nonsense as horseplay or smiling on the job.

Hall of Fame catcher Johnny Bench tracks this popup by Larry Biittner. One of many nice guys to play for the Cubs, Biittner is best remembered for losing a ball in his cap after sprawling in vain to make the catch.

Jay Brightens the Day

I didn't have to read Jay Johnstone's book, chock full of gags, practical jokes and one-liners, to realize I was dealing with a fun-loving guy. The former Cub and White Sox part-time outfielder and full-time prankster always has a glint in his eye, the one that keeps seeking another victim.

Regardless, it's impossible to get mad or stay annoyed with jovial Jay, even after your cap has been nailed to the dugout wall, your shoes filled with shaving cream or your locker packed with water-filled balloons. Johnstone was constantly on the lookout for gullible writers, too, so he figured he'd found a ripe pigeon—me—when our paths crossed in Comiskey Park while Jay was adding his colorful brand of color commentary to a televised White Sox game and I was trying to write a version coming somewhat closer to what really had happened.

We had been on friendly terms since 1972, when astute Sox general manager Roland Hemond swung a deal to bring the lefty swinger—and thinker—to Chicago. And when Jay got released without warning by the Cubs in 1984, after lightening their spirits and loosening up the rookies, I commiserated with him. But this was years later, and Jay had fresh mischief in mind, especially since illegal corking of bats by some players, notably Cleveland sourpuss Albert Belle, was a hot topic at the moment.

"Hey, Bob, you ought to go see [Sox trainer] Herm Schneider," Jay said. "He's in the clubhouse , talking about how Frank Thomas sneaks into the training room to put cork in his bat."

"Sure, Jay," I replied, fully aware he'd be disappointed when he picked up the paper the next morning, vainly seeking a screaming headline about the fictional bat-corking scandal.

That's just Jay's way. He and pitcher Jerry Reuss, a fellow free spirit, once delighted a Dodger Stadium crowd by trading their uniforms for goundskeepers' garb, joining the crew to sweep the infield between innings. He was the same old clubhouse cutup with the Cubs, easing the pressure of their 1984 playoff drive by asking fierce-looking reliever Lee Smith (actually a mild-mannered man): "Hey, Lee, why bother washing your car? Just glare at it and the dirt will fall off."

Bad Guy Makes Good

In his first stay with the Cubs, 1982 to 1984, pitcher Dickie Noles had other priorities besides pitching. Mainly, they were drinking, brawling and alienating teammates and sportswriters.

Along with a big-league fastball, Noles had a big-time attitude problem. He seemed bent on self-destruction, drowning his talent in an ocean of beer. Suddenly, after turning off most of the Chicago media with profane clubhouse tirades, the burly right-hander insisted he'd seen the light.

"I want to be a pitcher, not a drunk," Noles told one of his few friends, *Philadelphia Inquirer* sports editor Frank Dolson. What he didn't tell Dolson was that on bus trips to spring training games, Noles would hide in the bathroom, downing cans of beer slipped to him by a teammate.

Soon after the 1983 season started, Noles spent 15 days in jail for his role in a Cincinnati bar fight. Both his career and his life seemed to be heading straight down the drain. He was fortunate to find a savior in the Cubs' front office.

It was general manager Dallas Green, a gruff, no-nonsense type, not noted for sympathizing with troublemakers. Underneath that tough hide, though, Green had a soft spot for struggling young pitchers, perhaps because he had been one himself. A highly touted bonus rookie when he signed with the Phillies, Green got booed out of town by those ferocious Philadelphia fans. The lowlight of Green's career was serving up the 100th career home to Jimmy Piersall—whereupon Piersall celebrated by running around the bases backwards.

Green gave Noles two choices—go to an alcohol treatment program or get out. Noles made the right decision, pulling himself out of the gutter via a miraculous transformation. He changed, seemingly overnight, into a family man, a pleasant, soft-spoken, and above all, sober ballplayer. When Noles came back to the Cubs for a brief stint in 1987, he admitted that Green had saved his life.

"At first, the combination of booze and pitching in the majors was too much for me," Noles said. "Now if I drank, I'd be cheating myself. When I talk to kids, I tell them what I went through. It helps them understand they can choose the right direction for themselves."

Kingman Gets Crowned

Cubs fans can't say they weren't warned about Dave Kingman.

The strapping slugger was high on their villains list a year before he came to Chicago in 1978. He soon became the toast of the town, but adulation apparently was too hard to handle for him. A series of run-ins with the media, along with some depressingly dumb opinions in his ghostwritten newspaper columns, and King Kong was back on the fans' Get Lost list. That took some doing, because Kingman lit up Wrigley Field in 1979, leading both leagues with 48 homers, 25 of them in the Friendly Confines.

But there was no love lost on the North Side on Aug. 8, 1977, when the Cubs and Kingman's San Diego Padres got involved in a beanball brawl. Kingman picked the wrong target after taking a retaliatory plunk from Cub pitcher Steve Renko. Glaring, King Kong trudged to first base instead of charging the mound, a choice he soon regretted.

Sure enough, the next Padres hitter, George Hendrick, bounced a double play grounder to short and when second baseman Mick Kelleher took the throw, Kingman barreled into him with the best takeout block since the Packers' Jerry Kramer leveled the Cowboys' Jethro Pugh, opening the door for Bart Starr's legendary touchdown sneak on Green Bay's frozen tundra.

That got Kelleher's Irish up, so the five-foot-nine mighty mite leaped up and climbed Mt. Kingman, taking him down with a flying tackle. The ensuing melee was a dandy, wounding three Cubs—Kelleher, Jose Cardenal and Steve Ontiveros.

"It was a cheap shot," said Kelleher, nursing a sore neck and bruised ribs.

Kingman talked freely after that ambush, unlike the way he clammed up soon after joining his former antagonists a season later. In his version, the little guy was the aggressor.

"I didn't throw a punch," he lamented. "If I'd known the umpires were going to throw me out of the game, I would have gone right after Renko."

Despite his power at the plate, Kingman's chief legacy in Chicago consisted of opening an ice-cream parlor, dumping a bucket of water on a sportswriter, and tossing a female TV producer from his boat into Lake Michigan. When he demanded a hefty raise in 1980, the Cubs gladly shipped him to the New York Mets, presumably as revenge for 1969.

Mr. Clubhouse Cub

One of my favorite Cubs people never wore a uniform, but handled thousands of them. He's equipment manager Yosh Kawano, beginning his 61st year with the club. The Cubs dress in the Yosh Kawano Clubhouse, though he now handles a lighter load in the Wrigley Field visitors' bathhouse, upstairs on the first base side.

Kawano, a Wrigley fixture since 1943, has his name on the Cubs Walk of Fame as well as the clubhouse. In the tradition of Wrigley family loyalty, the 1981 sales contract to the Tribune Company assured his job for life. Yosh and I used to talk about golf, because he's a friend of touring pro

Raymond Floyd, but he politely declined any sort of personal publicity.

"I never won or lost a game for the Cubs, so why would anybody be interested in me?" he said.

Pepi Peps Up Cubs

For a few shining moments, Joe Pepitone sang a hit tune for the Cubs.

Sadly, Pepi's Wrigley Field rhapsody in 1970 did not turn out to be a long-playing record. His emotional temperament soon struck a sour note with maestro Leo Durocher, leader of the discordant Cubs band. Pepitone was the featured soloist, at least temporarily, but the whole Cubs orchestra sat on folding chairs.

It was a sad ending to the Durocher era, which had showed steady improvement since 1966, built up to a crashing 1969 crescendo and slowly disintegrated in the wake of that crushing defeat. At the end, Durocher and Pepitone, a pair of hot-tempered New York types, switched from Chicago buddies to exiled enemies.

By then, even the most rabid true believers in the Wrigley bleachers had to admit that Leo the Lip and Pepi the Hipster had outstayed both their welcome and their usefulness. It was the stuff of musical comedy, with an unhappy final act. Carmen Fanzone, a first-rate trumpet player and a second-rate third baseman, joined the Cubs just in time to blow taps over this sad affair.

Pepi arrived on Aug. 11, 1970, triggering an orgy of optimism for the struggling Cubs. His antics turned the clubhouse into Comedy Central, notably a side-splitting imitation of Marlon Brando's "I coulda been a contendah" scene from *On the Waterfront*. On the field, Pepi stirred up renewed pennant fever with fancy fielding and clutch hitting. Fans were entranced by his showbiz glamor, and he was quick to cash in with "Joe Pepitone's Thing," a swinging cabaret in the Rush Street night-life hub, plus a hair salon.

"This really is my kind of town," Pepi proclaimed, starring at his club nightly after doing so daily at the Friendly Confines.

Unfortunately, the fun and games failed to translate into winning games. The Cubs trailed NL East Division winner Pittsburgh at the end in 1970 and again in '71 and '72. By then, the Durocher-Pepitone love fest was deader than the short-lived hula hoop fad. Finger-pointing, blame-dodging and buck-passing replaced peace, harmony and other remnants of Pepi's hippie image.

So nobody was surprised when Pepitone announced that he was quitting, barely a month into the 1972 season. He came back briefly, but Durocher was gone soon after, leaving behind a trail of might-have-beens. Pepi hung around a bit longer, although when he left town for good in 1973, few fans bothered to notice or lament.

"Joe just had to do things his own way," said Ron Santo, Pepi's nightclub partner.

Chaw? Naw, Thanks

For old-time fans, the sight of Mark McGwire chomping a wad of gum and blowing a big bubble before stepping into the batter's box marked the end of an era. For me, too.

I recall going to Kansas City in 1980 to track George Brett's quest to become the first .400 hitter since Ted Williams. One more face in the media mob surrounding him nightly in the Royals' dugout did nothing to ease the pressure on Brett, who finished that year agonizingly short of his goal at .390. He had a quaint way of displaying his displeasure—spraying the writers' shoes with tobacco juice in an ever-widening circle.

It didn't bother me.

I can be numbered among the vanishing breed of diamond scribes who often left the park with tobacco-stained shoes. So I'm glad I wandered down to the Cubs' bullpen before a game in 1972 for a chat with reliever Steve Hamilton. The lanky left-hander was an authority on the theory and practice of The Chaw.

"My grandfather used to make the real stuff, so strong it would turn your hair gray," Hamilton said. "I've been chewing since I was 12. Now we have chewers like [fellow relief pitcher] Jack Aker, with finesse but no power. He spits straight down. Ralph Houk [Yankee manager] is a power chewer. It's not smart to get too close to him on a windy day. Rocky Bridges could do it all, but Les Peden would wrap his chaw in a napkin and take it out after lunch. He usually ate alone."

Hamilton was a Yankee teammate of Joe Pepitone. They both still chuckle about the day Hamilton blended his chaw and a big orange soda, with catastrophic results.

"I went out to the mound and couldn't stop barfing, in front of 30,000 people and a TV audience," Hamilton recalled. "Pepitone was laughing so hard, he fell off the dugout bench."

Jose, Can You Flee?

Jose Cardenal was one of my favorite Cubs. I wasn't alone, because Jose was always entertaining, even at his most exasperating. Either way, the colorful outfielder's niche in Cubs lore is secure, although he still denies two tales most often cited to illustrate Jose's unique style. One, repeated gleefully by Chicago media icon Mike Royko in his occasional columns about the joyfully hopeless lot of Cubs fans, had him sitting out an exhibition game because his eyelid got stuck shut. The other had Cardenal talking his way out of the lineup due to sleeplessness. It seems a cricket chirped under his bed all night, keeping him awake.

"None of that stuff ever happened," Cardenal told me once, angered by my factual report that he had run through a stop sign at third base, quashing a promising Cubs rally. "You writers think all Latin players are dumb."

Dumb, no. Crazy like a fox, yes. Cardenal knew how to play games with the media, and he enjoyed doing so. Mostly, the wiry little guy, just five foot ten and 160 pounds stripped, was a capable fielder, with surprising power at the plate and base-stealing speed. He also knew how to keep his name in print.

My personal tell-all—no, make that show-all—Cardenal escapade was in 1976. I was seated in manager Jim Marshall's clubhouse office, seeking nuggets to write about after a 2-0, two-hit Cubs loss. Cardenal's seventh-inning single broke up a budding no-hitter for the Giants' Ed Halicki, and he wanted to make sure we saw something to remember him by during the upcoming All-Star break.

So into the office strolled Jose, wearing only an oversized Mexican sombrero, to wish the writers a jolly holiday. Unfortunately, the photographers for all four Chicago papers already had departed, but how could anyone stay mad at a good-natured guy like that, especially *au naturel?*

Well, nobody except Herman Franks. When Marshall spun out of the Cubs' revolving managerial chair a year later, and the roly-poly Herman spun in, Cardenal's antics no longer got guffaws. Exiled to Philadelphia in a trade, Jose delighted in rekindling the feud, tormenting his ex-skipper by driving home seven runs in only 19 at-bats against the Cubs. When Franks gave the Phils' burly Bull Luzinski (later a flop for the White Sox in their 1984 playoff loss to Baltimore) an intentional pass to load the bases, Cardenal promptly emptied them, rifling a game-breaking double.

"All that hot dog knows how to do is cause trouble," Franks lamented.

Whatever he did, Jose got it done with crowd-pleasing flair.

Not-So-Wild Thing

The wildest thing about Mitch Williams was his control, not his velocity. Try as they might to turn this fireballing Cubs relief pitcher into a superflake, straight out of Ring Lardner's classic baseball satire *You Know Me Al,* it didn't work. Williams was a left-hander, adding more spice to the fictional web spun by some writers, anxious to turn Williams into the Cubs' counterpart to William "The Refrigerator" Perry of the Bears. That might not have been all bad, because Perry, an amiable young man, turned into an overnight millionaire, thanks to coach Mike Ditka's decision to let the hulking defensive tackle score a touchdown on national TV.

But Williams was neither a flake nor a southpaw version of Dizzy Dean, the loquacious Cardinals pitcher who cheerfully gave each interviewer several likely spots for his birthplace, along with a smorgasbord of conflicting, confusing anecdotes about his rise to stardom. Mainly, Mitch was a pleasant young guy, trapped on the media treadmill because he came along at a time when the Cubs were contenders.

I can still see him, slouching in a corner of the dugout, trying to say what he thought the pursuing array of pens, pencils, tape reorders and microphones wanted from him. Later, when the media crowd thinned, the Wild Thing could relax and gab about stuff he really enjoyed, such as bowling and riding motorcycles.

Williams racked up 36 saves while manager Don Zimmer steered the Cubs into the 1989 NL playoffs. The fireballing southpaw did it the hard way in his Wrigley Field debut on Opening Day, entering in the ninth inning to yield three singles. Then, with the bases full of Phillies and no outs, he did the wild thing, driving Cubs fans wild by striking out the side, including longtime Cub-killer Mike Schmidt, to preserve a 5-4 victory.

Control problems turned many of Williams's save situations into Perils-of-Pauline horsehide operas, with the hero surviving lots of self-inflicted peril, at least in 1989. Unfortunately, as so often happens in baseball, he soon self-destructed, plummeting from atop the heap to the bottom of the pile.

"I'm trying not to overthrow," said Williams, who threw over the heads of quaking hitters more often than over the plate throughout a 1990 season he wanted to throw out.

No wonder. Hobbled by a knee injury, the suddenly Mild Thing walked 50 in only 66 1/3 innings, getting raked for 60 hits in the process. His record was a dismal 1-8 that year, with his save total sliced in half to 18. Williams never did bounce all the way back, eventually drifting to Philadelphia, where his career imploded with a cataclysm that gave renewed credence to the Big Bang theory. Ex-Cub Joe Carter set off a wild explosion in Toronto by nuking Williams's last pitch of the 1993 World Series over the fence in Game 6, giving the Blue Jays the second walk-off, Series-winning homer in Fall Classic annals. The other one? Bill Mazeroskis 1960 ninth-inning, seventh-game blast to stun the Yankees.

As always, Williams refused to alibi or hide from the media after that game. He admitted his confidence was shot and that his control probably deserved the same fate.

Much Too Frank

Stormy sojourns are nothing new for the Cubs. Neither is political incorrectness. Going all the way back to ancient history, the 19th century, their Hall of Fame player-manager, Cap Anson, refused to take the field against teams with black players in their lineup. No storms of protest greeted his stand, because that's the way it was then in baseball and most of American society.

But when temperamental Cubs pitcher Julian Taverez opened his mouth and inserted his foot, he picked both the wrong time and the wrong place. Enraged by heckling from fans at San Francisco's Pac Bell Park on April 28, 2001, the right-hander erupted after a tough 2-1 loss to the Giants. Angrily shrugging off the booing he got throughout the game, he went totally off his John Rocker.

"These fans are *bleeps* and *bleeps*," Tavarez fumed, refusing to retract his derogatory terms for gay men and women, even though onlookers warned him such language would stir up a storm in San Francisco, a haven for alternative lifestyles.

Not since Cubs manager Lee Elia roasted Wrigley Field fans ("They can kiss my *bleep*") 18 years earlier, on April 29, 1983, had a postgame tantrum backfired so badly The reaction to Tavarez's childish fit of pique was so harsh that Cubs manager Don Baylor had to kick off damage-control efforts almost immediately. Baylor sat down with the native of the Dominican Republic and put his freedom of speech on a short leash, something totally at odds with Tavarez's tendency to shoot from the lip.

So phase one of the spin solution began when Tavarez held court the next day with Chicago and San Francisco writers. Basically, the baffled pitcher used the same defense Dizzy Dean employed when Cards manager Frankie Frisch jumped him after the colorful pitcher got picked off first base.

"Frankie, I musta gone into a transom," Dean said.

Because there was no way to deny his words, especially after they became the lead story, even on network news broadcasts, all Tavarez could do was backpedal.

"I didn't mean it," he said. "My emotions got in the way, and I'm totally sorry. I want to apologize to San Francisco and the Cubs and everybody who was offended by what I said."

Anxious to avoid another John Rocker-style uproar, commissioner Bud Selig's office issued a tut-tut, tsk-tsk statement, along with the obligatory suspension for Tavarez, plus a fine, donated to organizations serving the groups he had slurred. As soon as they could, the Cubs unloaded Tavarez, the same fate that had befallen Elia soon after his 1983 outburst.

Hard-Luck Buckner

Nobody could question Bill Buckner's work ethic. His judgment? That's another matter. An intense, competitive guy, Buckner hustled, scrapped and clawed for everything, sometimes too hard.

He was a big-league hitter for eight eventful Cub seasons (1977-84), but his ego got him into frequent hot water. His image got pummeled by a series of strange escapades, notably a deserved mauling in 1982 from Cubs manager Lee Elia after Buckner called pitcher Dan Larson "a gutless so-and-so." It happened on the bench during a game in—where else?—San Diego, with TV cameras relaying the blow-by-blow to Chicago for a late, late show.

Buckner and Herman Franks also got into a remarkably silly name-calling contest when the Cubs' manager stepped down in 1979. Mainly, they served to reinforce the notion that some ballplayers are overgrown, as well as overpaid, kids, exchanging taunts on the playground.

"Buckner goes nuts if he doesn't get a hit every game, regardless if the Cubs won or lost," Franks snorted. "Herman's a fat clown," Buckner retorted.

Hitless or not, handsome Buckner was a hit with female fans. Even hard-core bleacherites admired the way he played through the pain of ankle operations and assorted injuries. They all would have turned on him, though, if Buckner had told them what he really thought of Wrigley Field before leaving town.

"I hate this place," he confessed. "Wrigley Field plays with your mind, especially when the wind blows in day games. That's practically all the time. It's the worst place in baseball, but the fans are great."

Hill of a Blast

Did Glenallen Hill propel the longest-ever Wrigley Field home run? And did it really soar 451.2 feet, as the *Chicago Sun-Times* claimed after hiring surveyors to track Hill's titanic clout on May 11, 2000?

That was a little less than the 490-foot distance estimated by the Cubs at the time Hill unloaded on a delivery from Steve Woodard of the Milwaukee Brewers. And a lot less than Hill figured.

"Hey, I hit that ball 700 feet," the muscular outfielder said.

One glance at Hill's bulging biceps could have convinced some of us overweight, out-of-shape diamond scribes that he was capable of propelling a pitch into nearby Lake Michigan, if the fickle Wrigley winds happened to be blowing toward the fences. Whatever the distance, it was a formidable poke, clearing the screen in back of the left-field bleachers, soaring majestically across Waveland Avenue and bouncing on the roof of a brick apartment building across the street.

How far it went, or would have gone if it had landed unimpeded, is anyone's guess. That's just fine with the trio of Cubs employees who list homer distances on the scoreboard. Wayne Messmer, the golden-throated vocalist who turns his rendition of the Nation Anthem into an instant July 4th celebration, huddles with his co-PA announcer, Paul Friedman, and Gary Pressy, the Wrigley Field organist. On homers hit into the stands, they add three feet of distance for each row deeper. But Hill's homer, Messmer cheerfully agrees, will remain a Cubs trivia topic and a matter of conjecture for the bleacher creatures and all Cub fans. It should give Hill a convincing argument whenever ex-Cubs gather to rehash all those strange goings-on in the Friendly Confines. Every year, as Cubs Hall of Famer Billy Williams pointed out, "All our homers get 100 feet longer."

With or without the extra distance, Hill qualifies as a Cubs character, even though he wasn't around all that long in two separate stints during the '90s. He liked to hold court in the clubhouse, pontificating on a potpourri of subjects, always with his short-sleeved T-shirt rolled up to display those Mike Tyson-sized arm muscles. When Hill slammed a 3-0 pitch from Mets closer John Franco for a game-winning pinch homer on July 26, 1988, he was ready for the postgame media invasion.

"I don't think I can hit a ball harder than that one," he said of the payoff shot into the center field bleachers. "Just like a snake layin' in the weeds, I was ready."

But Hill's defensive liabilities made him expendable, so a week after Cubs president Andy MacPhail tapped himself to replace embattled general manager Ed Lynch, Hill got dealt to the Yankees on July 21, 2000 for a couple of minor-leaguers.

"If I start reflecting on my Chicago memories, you'll see a 235-pound man cry," was Hill's farewell salute.

CHAPTER 3

CUBBIE BLUE, WE LOVE YOU

Cubs fans come in all shapes, sizes, ages, sexes, nationalities, races and occupations, irrespective of social class, high school class or total lack of class. It's a wholly democratic (Republicans allowed, too) equal-opportunity fraternity, dedicated to the proposition that all Cubs fans are created equal, with the same virtually limitless capacity for frustration. Regardless of where they come from, this band of brothers and sisters comes together every year on Opening Day, united in the belief that the unbeaten Cubs will stay that way—at least until later that afternoon.

Wealth and status can't inoculate anyone with an antidote to Cub Fever, a rampaging virus that's been known to bring Chicago (except for stubborn pockets of South Side immunity) to its knees. Fan clubs run the same eclectic gamut, from the snobby Emil Verban Society, mostly a bunch of power-lunching Washington, D.C. dilettantes, to the Wild Bunch, a band of beer-guzzling diehards hanging out at Bernie's saloon, right across Clark Street from the ballpark. The most famous group of all was the Left Field Bleacher Bums, emerging in the late '60s to swear allegiance to Cubs manager Leo Durocher and swear at anyone fearless or foolish enough to trample on Wrigley's sacred turf while wearing the uniform of a visiting team. Standards have changed in America since the 1960s—unhappily, not for the better—so the verbal, and perhaps actual, bile dumped on opponents by the Bums was not nearly as vile as the language hurled at them nowadays, even from some box-seat bellowers.

Still, the Bleacher Bums' exploits became the stuff of Wrigleyville legend, and some of the outrageous stunts attributed to them actually did happen. Just like the lengths of players' homers after they retire, stories of malicious mischief in the bleachers tend to escalate with the passing years. Through it all, though, the constant element has been the unswerving, undying loyalty of Cubs fans. Together or singly, in packs or slacks or cutoff jeans or bare-chested (this brand of ultimate fan is all male, at least so far), the Wrigley royal rooters keep coming, keep hoping and keep soaking up the magnificent mixture of suds and sunshine that annually adds new chapters to the lore—and lure—of Wrigley Field.

Moody Movement

I f the Cubs win, the mood is lighter and so is the exit traffic. Cubs fans linger longer in their seats, savoring the sunshine and what Jack Brickhouse used to call the "happy totals" on the center field scoreboard. A totally different karma fills the air, as noticeable as the fog that sometimes shrouds the place in spring or fall, if the Cubs lose. In that event, the exodus tends to be quicker and gloomier. Instead of departing with loud, surly second-guesses of their team's misfortune, Cubs fans seem to exhale a collective sigh of regret, trudging out in resigned silence.

Soon after, their irrepressible optimism triggers the bounce-back process, sometimes within minutes. Before they reach home, the friendly confines of the Cubby Bear Lounge, Bernie's Saloon or some other Wrigleyville oasis, the real diehards are already regenerating the optimism that seems to be the native state and lifelong fate of Cubs fans. Over the years, I've heard them say basically the same thing again and again, in slightly different terms, on the way out of Wrigley Field:

"I wish the Cubs had better [hitting, pitching, fielding, or whatever combination was lacking that day], but this is a great place to see a game."

One Big Hopeful Family

Cubs fans agree their affliction is a terminal disease. Highly contagious, too. It's passed along from grandfathers and grandmothers to moms and dads to sons and daughters and on and on, with no discernable generation gap. Whenever I hear bunches of them talking among themselves, the dialogue is strikingly similar to the same stuff emerging from the mouths of 1969 survivors. Those fans didn't blame the players then. Now, more than three decades later, the voices of former Bleacher Bums still ooze nostalgia when they recall that smooth-as-silk infield—Ernie Banks, Glenn Beckert, Don Kessinger, Ron Santo—Sweet Swinger Billy Williams, fiery catcher Randy "Rebel" Hundley, or pitchers Fergie Jenkins, Ken Holtzman and bullpen cutup Dick Selma.

Gabby About Babe

A longtime Cubs fan named Bob Callahan was one of the fortunate few to be connected personally with the two most famous home runs in Wrigley Field's storied history. Younger Cubs fans will talk about Sammy Sosa's historic 60th and 61st homers, both at the Friendly Confines on the same day, September 13, 1998. They also savor Slammin' Sammy's September 18, 1999, blast off teammate-to-be Jason Bere, making him the first big-leaguer ever to swat 60 home runs in two seasons.

Others can't forget the hysteria triggered by Gary Gaetti's clutch two-run homer on September 28, 1998, sending the Cubs to a 5-3 victory over San Francisco. The Cubs and Giants met in a Wrigley Field first that night—a one-game playoff for the NL wild card berth. Cubs fans celebrated the victory as though their team had just won a World Series game, though any chance of that got snuffed out in a three-game Atlanta Braves sweep in the first round of the playoffs.

Or how about Ryne Sandberg's back-to-back home runs in the ninth and 10th innings on June 23, 1984? Ryno's heroics earned the ultimate tribute from Cards manager Whitey Herzog: "Here comes Baby Ruth." Throw in Willie Smith's two-run pinch homer in the 11th inning on Opening

Day, 1969—Jack Brickhouse's personal favorite—to beat the Phillies, 7-6. And the three straight round-trippers by Karl "Tuffy" Rhodes of the Cubs on Opening Day, 1994.

But the real Babe Ruth stands tallest on the list for his "called shot" World Series homer. In Game 3, on October 1, 1932, Ruth swaggered to the plate in the fifth inning, pointed to the center field bleachers and parked Cubs pitcher Charlie Root's next serve in that spot, sending the Yankees toward a 4-0 sweep. Of course, diehard Cubs fans insist that catcher-manager Gabby Hartnett's celebrated Homer in the Gloaming, as darkness shrouded Wrigley Field on September 28, 1938, was more important. It beat Pittsburgh, 6-5, and put the Cubs in first place, enabling them to edge the Pirates in a tight NL pennant race.

That's where Bob Callahan comes in. He was a Wrigley Field spectator for Ruth's called shot, insisting that's exactly what the Bambino did.

"I saw Babe point to the stands and hit the ball where he said he would," Callahan related.

Years later, Callahan told me of the day he played golf with Hartnett, who was behind the plate for the Cubs in that '32 World Series. Both men agreed it was too dark to play ball in Wrigley Field when Gabby connected for his all-time clutch Cub homer in 1938. When asked if Ruth really pointed with his bat toward the bleachers, as Callahan and some Wrigley Field spectators swore he did—while others, including Root, swore he didn't—Hartnett merely smiled.

"We're talking about Babe Ruth here," the Hall of Fame catcher said. "Some people like to tear down legends, but I'm not one of them."

Raising the Roof

Short of hitting the Illinois Lottery jackpot, one of the best investments in the last quarter-century has been Wrigleyville real estate. This little slice of turf, about one square mile, nestled inside a Chicago neighborhood called Lake View, became a gold mine for some speculators along with individual investors. The mother lode of this bonanza sits on one block of Waveland Avenue and another on Sheffield Avenue. These fortunate three-flats offer a view of Cubs games from their rooftops—Waveland behind the left field bleachers and Sheffield in center and right. Who knew, back when economic times were tough in the mid-70s and the Cubs' self-imposed postseason boycott stretched on year after year that those aging apartments would become cash-cow centers of controversy?

Buildings that sold for just over $80,000 in that era now are worth millions, embroiled in legal warfare with the Tribune Company over their right to sell rooftop seats for Cubs games. It's trendy to roost up there, so the in-crowd snaps up those outside perches, the ultimate in viewer chic, paying more than they would to get inside Wrigley Field. Responding to a lawsuit filed by the Cubs, alleging that rooftop owners "unjustly enrich themselves," 13 of the landlords pointed out that they've been licensed by the city of Chicago since 1998, paying taxes on the big bucks they rake in. The ongoing court battle delayed plans to enlarge the bleachers, another prestige place for Cubs fans to park their fannies.

"Roof rights" to some buildings with a view are owned by a company which rents to groups throwing upscale—and upstairs—tailgate parties for as much as $10,000 per

Rooftop fans across the street from Wrigley Field watch an enemy homer soar toward them. They're used to dodging brickbats in the legal battle with the Cubs over the big bucks people pay to see games from those perches.

game. That includes catering service and an open bar. Single rooftop tickets can go for more than $100, higher on weekends.

Verban to Reagan to White House

E mil Verban played in one World Series during his undistinguished big-league career. It was in 1944, a year before the Cubs made their final 20th-century appearance in the Fall Classic. Verban made the most of his one shot, batting a hefty .417 on seven singles in 17 trips—better than Stan Musial's .304—in pacing the Cards to a six-game victory over the Browns, the only all-St. Louis World Series. By the time the second baseman got to the Cubs in 1948, the postseason was only a fond memory for him and them.

Verban did stroke his only homer in the majors as a Cub, ending his career with one for 2,911 in the round-tripper column.

So it seemed fitting for an exclusive band of Cubs fans, including former President Ronald Reagan, to label themselves the Emil Verban Society. Reagan, who recreated Cubs games via Western Union ticker for radio station WHO in Des Moines during the 1930s, hosted Verban at a White House meeting of his fan club. Cubs fans really do come in all shapes, sizes, social strata and political persuasions.

Dr. Ernie Prescribes...

When Ernie Banks visited the 2003 Cubs fan convention, he got the same riotous reception they give him whenever and wherever the Hall of Fame shortstop/first baseman appears. In between signing autographs on caps, his familiar No. 14 jersey and just about anything thrust at him by older fans, who remember him well, and younger ones, who never saw him play, Mr. Cub reflected on today's changing expectations.

"Even Cubs fans can't live only on love any more," Banks told me. "They need to be rewarded by watching a winning team. In my career, just playing in front of those Wrigley Field rooters every day was like being in the World Series. Their loyalty to the Cubs made me feel the same way toward them and Mr. [Phil] Wrigley, who did everything he could to bring Chicago a winner.

"So the way they stuck with us, win or lose, mattered more than anything else. But times have changed. The fans today want success."

And Some Want Excess

Banks was right on both counts. New Age Cubs fans might not totally share the win-or-else fervor sweeping through all sports at all levels, but they're much less willing to accept mediocrity. And Wrigley Field, for decades an oasis of tranquility in a tidal wave of fan upheaval, now has to deal with occasional outbursts from rowdies in the stands. The ugliest incident in recent years erupted on

May 17, 2000, in the ninth inning of a 6-5 Cubs loss to the Dodgers.

In a nutshell, heckling directed at the visitors' bullpen escalated into throwing hot dog buns, not-entirely-empty beer cups and eventually punches at the Dodgers sitting there, with their backs to the stands. One of the victims, ex-White Sox catcher Chad Kreuter, got punched in the head while his cap was being stolen. Kreuter made an unwise decision, chasing the capnapper into the stands, followed by truculent teammates, to trigger a fist-swinging brawl. Fortunately, no skulls got fractured, although the inevitable aftermath was another battle royale of conflicting finger-pointing and blame-dodging. It was followed by hefty fines and suspensions for Los Angeles players and coaches involved in the melee, plus cash settlements for alleged injuries to other participants.

The major victim was Wrigley Field's time-honored tradition of harmless fun at the old ballpark. With heightened security and more restrictions on fan access to the players, the Friendly Confines began to look a little like Fort Wrigley—an outcome deplored by the vast majority of real Cubs fans.

"It's hard to put a happy face on things like this," admitted Cubs president Andy MacPhail. "I hope this is not the new reality, but whatever it is, we have to deal with it."

Rocker and Rolling

Actually, not much fan unrest in this new era of victory celebrations often marked by overturned, burning cars and shattered store windows was first seen in or around Wrigley Field. The genteel family and fan-friendly tradition of the Wrigley family, especially P. K.'s insistence on having 15,000 or more seats for sale on game days, had something to do with that. So did the obvious charm of their ballpark, a place that blended the relaxed atmosphere of a summer picnic with baseball.

In my first 20 years of Cubs coverage, it's hard to recall much violence, aside from the sort perpetrated by visiting hitters on Cubs pitchers when the wind blew out. Before then, even with the winds of change blowing across America, sparking upheaval and unrest during the Vietnam war, Cubs fans were too busy celebrating the excitement of self-proclaimed managerial genius Leo Durocher's bid to win pennants.

Leo the Lip made a lot of noise, but couldn't steer a star-studded team into the playoffs. The late fade of 1969 shaped the attitudes of many young Cubs fans, tempering their diehard loyalty with a blend of resigned reality

But Wrigley Field's idyllic image could not hold out forever. Jack Brickhouse's mellow voice got replaced by Harry Caray's rallying cry—"You can't beat fun at the old ballpark!" Harry certainly was not a member of the MTV generation, and his passion was baseball, not the Woodstock lifestyle. Regardless, the gap between older and younger fans on the definition of "fun" widened considerably, resulting in a few escapades that raised eyebrows in and out of Wrigleyville. Unruly conduct sometimes went beyond the innocent fun of Yuppie-style streakers dashing harmlessly, if revealingly, through the outfield.

The Beef Goes On

Cubs fans weren't whistling "Dixie" when John Rocker slouched into Wrigley Field on May 29, 2000. It was Memorial Day, but what everybody remembered on this visit was the way the loose-lipped pitcher had opened his mouth and inserted his foot, displaying monumental stupidity.

The closer for the Atlanta Braves almost closed his own career by unleashing a tirade against various minorities and even one of his own teammates. It appeared in *Sports Illustrated*, earning Rocker a hefty fine and suspension and baseball some unwelcome publicity. Understandably, beefed-up security forces were on full alert wherever the Braves went after Rocker returned to their bullpen. That was especially true in Wrigley Field, still reeling from the charge of the Dodger Blue brigade into the stands less than two weeks earlier.

That altercation had broken out in the same right field bullpen area where Rocker took a seat with the Braves' relief crew. In the interim, beer sales were cut off earlier, chug-a-lugs per customer limited and area vendors reduced, so thirsty would-be hecklers at least would have to walk off some of their alcohol-induced ire. Kevin Hallinan, baseball's boss cop, was in Wrigley Field for Rocker's appearance, an indication that commissioner Bud Selig believed both the game and the rowdy fans got a black eye in the Dodger rumble.

"The commissioner could end all that by ruling any player who goes into the stands for any reason automatically gets suspended for one year," prescribed Atlanta manager Bobby Cox.

The Braves' skipper had no way of knowing he'd be thrown off the field, while Rocker sat it out peacefully, for harassing the umps. Neither man was needed, because ex-Cub Greg Maddux tormented his old team, 1-0. Pitching in typical tough luck, Cubs starter Jon Lieber spun a perfect game until Andres Galarraga's two-out homer in the seventh inning.

The Roar of '84

The Cubs' collapse in San Diego, where they struck out three straight times to end that agonizing NL Championship Series right where they started—one game short of the World Series—was the true test of their fans' mettle. Of all the painful episodes in baseball history, that weekend has to rank up there with the worst.

Before the crash, the Cubs and their fans were flying high. Just like the Super Bowl-bound Bears did a year later, the players recorded their version of the "Super Bowl Shuffle." The baseball rendition was a country-western foot-stomper called "Men in Blue," with Rick Sutcliffe, Jody Davis, Leon Durham, Keith Moreland and Gary Woods vocalizing. A few lines from the lyrics:

"It's been a long time since 1945, but the Wrigley Field faithful always kept the spirit alive,

"And now's the time and here's the place we even up the score,

"The hopes are high, the pennant will fly over Wrigley in '84,

"And as sure as there's ivy on the center field wall, the men in blue are going to win it all."

That prediction by those Tribune Company employees proved just as accurate as the *Chicago Tribune's* banner headline—"Dewey Defeats Truman"—about the outcome of the 1948 presidential election. The Cubs led in the standings, just like Thomas E. Dewey led in the polls, but victory predictions for both turned out to be monumental goofs. At least, the losing 1984 Cubs evoked an outpouring of sympathy in Chicago and all over America. Harry Caray's flamboyant style made him a household word—and the Cubs household faces—all over the country.

"People have adopted the Cubs," Caray told me during that upbeat season. "The ones living far away can't get to Chicago, so they show up in Atlanta, Houston, Cincinnati or wherever we play, holding up bedsheets and banners with the Cub logo, wearing Cub hats and waving Cub pennants. If I read all the Go-Cubs notes they send to the TV booth, I wouldn't have time to broadcast the game."

Fans Fan the Flame

In the end, just about the only people not waving a 1984 pennant were the Cubs themselves. Regardless, Cubs fans refused to give up on them after that playoff disaster. Ditto for the playoff setbacks of 1989 and 1998. Adversity seems only to toughen their battered hides and renew their weary spirits. One of the most remarkable things about Cubs loyalists, to me at least, is the way they seem frozen in time.

The rest of the country and the whole world, for that matter, changes by the minute in rapid-fire sequences. Yet the way these people feel about their baseball team, and the pleasure they derive from sticking with it, win, lose or tie, remains the same. I honestly don't know why, but any objective observer would have to conclude Cubs fans are the blue-ribbon champions of undying, although not always unquestioning, loyalty.

They Love Ivy and Sammy

Maybe the most remarkable thing about Cubs fans is the way they express their emotional attachment. Almost universally, it's evenly divided between Wrigley Field and the players. That equation never seems to change. Every time I start to write a book about the Cubs, I dig out notebooks, scraps of paper and dog-eared scorecards with quotes from fans, going all the way back to 1970. Other files, newspaper clips and similar sources, some as far back as the World Series of 1908—their last 20th-century postseason victory—contain remarkably similar sentiments about the players of that era.

But almost as soon as the Cubs moved into Weeghman Park in 1916, the place that's been home to them ever since, the players had a rival for the affection of their supporters. It was the ballpark, where fans have remained so close to the action that they can relate to it more than anywhere else. I went to the 2003 Cubs Convention to see if a new generation of fans had emerged to salute the dawn of the Dusty Baker era. Here's what I found:

One of my all-time favorite Cubs fans was there early, waiting patiently for encouraging words from new manager Baker, anxious for some autographs and ever-hopeful that the breakthrough year is at hand, at last. He's Casey Knapp,

A little divine intervention is always welcome at Wrigley Field. Sister Josephine Maynard leaves no doubt she's rooting the Cubs to victory.

a wheelchair-bound youngster from Lake Geneva, Wisconsin, who qualifies as a Cubs fanatic in all categories, especially optimism. And like most of the conventioneers, his affection is equally divided between Wrigley Field, Sammy Sosa and any other bodies draped in Cubbie Blue.

"It's such a fan-friendly ballpark," Casey said of Wrigley. "Going to a game there is more fun."

Wayne Wysocki grew up on the South Side, but now lives in Munster, Indiana, closer to Chicago's Loop than some Northwest suburbs. He's living proof that geography is no impediment to Cubmania.

"White Sox fans were all around us when I was a kid," Wysocki said. "But my Dad was a Cub fan and he made sure I turned into one. I guess there's no way you can stop rooting for the team that Ernie Banks played for."

Charlotte Santore and Carol Berg live in far-apart suburbs, but shared affection for the Cubs lures these longtime friends to the ballpark. So does a chance for close-up looks at their favorite players in skin-tight double-knit pants.

"I love the park and I miss Mark Grace," Berg said. "The way he dug throws out of the dirt at first base saved Shawon Dunston a lot of errors, and he's a good-looking guy."

"Going to Wrigley Field is always exciting," Santore chimed in. "It's a great way to spend an afternoon, even when the Cubs don't win."

Individual touches on Cubs attire enable fans to add some style to their rooting. Heads swivel in the stands whenever the guys from Kenosha, Wisconsin, show up wearing their snappy Cubs caps adorned with moose ears. They claim it's a tribute to Moose Moryn, the outfielder who saved Don Cardwell's Wrigley Field no-hitter on May 15, 1960, with a diving, two-out catch in the ninth inning. Whatever, Bill Chase, Greg Picazo, Bob Rubeck, Jeff Galligan and all that gang are certified Cubs maniacs. So are Phil Ertel and his three sons, posing for pictures in their Cubs shirts after driving from Cary, North Carolina, to soak up more Cubs lore.

Cub One, Cub All

They come in all shapes and sizes, from everywhere under the sun. The old Die-Hard Fan Club and yesteryear's hangout, Ray's Bleachers, have been replaced by today's Wild Bunch, which hangs out at Bernie's bar. The names and faces change, but Cubs loyalty exists, persists and refuses to desist. The way it is gets summed up for all of them by Deborah Martinez, a true blue North Sider.

"Take the Cubbies out of Wrigley Field and it wouldn't be the same," she said. "If they played in a new stadium, I'd have to go see them, but it wouldn't be as much fun."

Yes, you can't beat fun and sun or moon, day or night, in this old ballpark.

CHAPTER 4

TOWERS OF CUBS POWER

The Cubs have enough Hall of Fame performers, past, present and future, to keep them busy polishing plaques. Their own Walk of Fame, moved inside Wrigley Field to make space for all those tributes to the growing list of memorable Cubs, adds a pleasant pregame trip to the tradition that bonds generations of fans.

So far, 41 Hall of Famers with at least some Cub connections adorn the walls of the baseball museum in Cooperstown, N.Y. That group will grow when second baseman Ryne Sandberg joins the lodge. I was surprised, although not shocked, when Ryno didn't make it in 2003, his first turn on the ballot.

Members of the Baseball Writers Association of America are eligible to vote after covering the big leagues for 10 years, a chore I take seriously. Almost assuredly, Sammy Sosa will enter the Hall on the first ballot when his brilliant career ends.

Ron Santo belongs, as well, because he passed the major test of consistently outstanding performance at third base and at bat for the Cubs. I'm surprised the Old Timers committee didn't let him join Cubs buddies Ernie Banks, Billy Williams and Fergie Jenkins in 2003. Pitchers Lee Smith and Bruce Sutter, along with outfielder Andre Dawson, spent significant parts of their careers with the Cubs, and all three are good bets to get there sooner or later. Among the serious candidates now eligible for the Hall of Fame, pitcher Rich "Goose" Gossage had more success with the White Sox and other teams, so Cubs fans don't consider him one of their own.

Long Road Ahead

It's too early to tell whether the potential of Cubs right-handers Kerry Wood and Mark Prior will translate into enough victories to make them viable candidates, especially with the arm trouble that seems to plague all hard-throwing pitchers. But Cubs fans have their own Hall of Fame. Such longtime favorites as Santo, "Hawk" Dawson, catcher Randy "The Rebel" Hundley, pitchers Rick Sutcliffe and Rick Reuschel and shortstop Don Kessinger might not make it to Cooperstown, but their fame is secure in Wrigleyville. Real Cubs fans tend to go for players fitting the tradition and lifestyle of Wrigley Field—gamers who enjoy the ivy on the walls and the electricity of this unique ballpark.

Two classy right-handers, Greg Maddux and Jon Lieber, would have qualified. Sadly, Maddux fled to Atlanta when the Cubs wouldn't pay him what he was worth—a Chicago sports blunder rivaled only by the Blackhawks letting Bobby Hull get away in 1972—and arm woes cut short Lieber's stay. Still, superstars are much more plentiful than pennants for the Cubs, especially since 1945. For instance:

Sammy Slammin'

L ike legendary muscleman Samson, Cubs powerman Sammy Sosa has been carrying the weight of the world on his shoulders. Sosa's world is baseball and his domain is Wrigley Field, where he reigns as Chicago's most popular sports figure since Michael Jordan sounded taps over the Bulls' six-peat NBA dynasty of the '90s by moving to Washington.

"Sammy was kind of a wild kid in his younger days," said Gene Lamont, who had just been named White Sox manager in 1992 when Sosa got traded to the Cubs. "I could see he'd be good eventually, but nobody thought he could hit 60 homers or become the superstar he is now."

Sosa's first Sox manager, Jeff Torborg, got a glimpse of that raw, untapped potential. In his 1989 Sox debut against the Twins, Sosa lashed a two-run homer, a pair of singles and even walked twice.

"Sammy swung at a lot of ball-four pitches and dropped some catchable fly balls, but you could see all that ability, just waiting to come out," Torborg said. "Now he's baseball's best ambassador."

What made the difference for Sosa was his willingness to work on his weaknesses. He made himself into an adequate, if not spectacular, guardian of Wrigley Field's tricky patch of right-field turf, learning how to cope with glaring sun and treacherous winds. It was as a hitter, though, that Sosa made giant strides, electrifying the entire country with his titanic 1998 home run duel that the Cards' Mark McGwire eventually won, 70-66.

The fact that Sosa by then clearly was the people's choice, at least outside of St. Louis, proved how far he had come, both as a ballplayer and a man. At the home run derby before the '98 All-Star Game in the Colorado Rockies' Coors Field, Sosa was the life of the party, heckling his peers and charming the fans.

His incredible June of 1998, a 20-homer rampage that smashed all long-distance records for a single month, propelled Sosa to international celebrity status, and he's been riding that multimedia horse ever since.

Some breathless pundits actually tapped Sosa and McGwire as baseball's twin saviors because they bashed a combined 136 homers in their fence-busting derby. That was more than a slight exaggeration, although both sluggers spun a merry turnstile tune everywhere they went, diminishing some leftover fan enmity from the bitter strike-walkout that erased the 1994 World Series.

If personality made the difference, Sosa would have won in a walk, intentional or otherwise. While McGwire mumbled "I feel like a caged animal" about the adulation every fan would have sold his soul to George Steinbrenner for, Smilin' Sammy seemed to be having the time of his life. He probably was.

"June changed everything," Sosa told me about that homer-happy binge. "It all fell into place and I did something

Sammy Sosa keeps adding to the career totals that virtually assure him a first-ballot Hall of Fame berth.

Babe Ruth or nobody else has done, without feeling any
pressure."

Wood He Kerry the Cubs?

Yes, he Wood—if he could. Cubs fans can't help
wondering what might have been if Kerry Wood's
right arm, perhaps the deadliest weapon in Chicago sports
since Bobby Hull's slap shot, had stayed sound.

It didn't, of course. Wood missed all of 1999 to recover
from Tommy John surgery on a torn ligament in his right
elbow. Many Cubs fans feel that if only Wood was a trifle
less competitive and more willing just to pick up a paycheck,
instead of playing hurt, things could have been different.
That's not Wood. His insistence on starting Game 3 of the
1998 NL playoff with Atlanta, despite that ailing elbow,
was a bad decision, but the one he wanted to make. For the
Cubs and Wood, that raw, windy night was another Wrigley
Field reenactment of Custer's last stand.

Obviously toiling, Wood somehow pitched a gritty five
innings, yielding just one run on three hits—and still lost,
completing a three-game sweep for the Braves. Could it be
that Wood's most magnificent moment, a 20-strikeout
Wrigley whitewash of the Houston Astros on May 6, 1998,
triggered the damage that forced the right-hander to undergo
career-threatening surgery the following spring?

A chart of Wood's 122 pitches (84 for strikes) in that
awesome effort clocked more than 30 of his fastballs at 95-
plus miles per hour, with a couple of them at or above 100
MPH. For a 20-year-old kid in his first big-league season,

even this muscular phenom, elbow-wrenching curves and sliders take more of a toll than than unhittable heat.

Wood doesn't want to talk about such stuff. Mainly, he wants to pitch—and win—for the Cubs.

"I don't want to make excuses," he said. "The Cubs haven't been winning, and I take my share of responsibility. Our fans won't stop hoping, no matter how much we let them down."

Wood's struggles, especially with control, since he came back to the starting rotation in 1999 have been frustrating. Mixed with flashes of true greatness, he's had wild spells, walking too many batters and falling behind in the count to others. Even pitchers with Wood's smoke get burned when they have to throw fastballs over the plate.

Now comes the year of decision for Wood. He'll be 26 on June 16, 2003, heading toward the halfway point of his fifth big-league season. It's the time when pitchers with his kind of stuff—and heart—reach their prime. This might be, could be, maybe even Wood be, the jumpoff point for his string of 20-victory seasons—if there are to be any.

No Prior Restraint

Kerry Wood might have thought he was watching a Wrigley Field videotape on May 22, 2002. At times, this looked like a rerun of K-K-K-Kerry's demolition job on Houston four seasons earlier. Well, not quite.

Cubs rookie Mark Prior struck out a mere 10 Pittsburgh Pirates in six innings, only half of Wood's total against the Astros. And this game was at night, unlike the sunlit afternoon that seemed to be lighting up Wood's can't-miss

Hall of Fame prospects. Regardless, Prior showed the same sort of unlimited potential on this eye-opening spring evening that had been displayed by Wood on his 20-K day.

Bleacher fans got just as excited, too, pinning those paper Ks up on the back screen as Prior's total swelled. At last, the Cubs boasted No. 1 and No. 1-A starters to trot out for Dusty Baker's 2003 managerial debut. They're both right-handers with level heads and crackling fastballs. All the Cubs can do is hope Prior doesn't have to face the misfortune that pared a year off Wood's career, to mend from elbow surgery.

For his part, Prior didn't bring the typical rookie's "Gulp, gee whiz" demeanor up to the majors with him. Even a cool customer like Wood confessed that his knees were shaking when he took the Wrigley Field mound for the first time in 1998. Not Prior.

"I've pitched under pressure," said the 2001 national college Player of the Year after beating the Pirates 7-4 in his Cub debut. "I didn't feel pressure tonight. Pitchers should concentrate on winning every inning, because that 's the way to win every start. If you keep your mind on that, there's no time to get distracted."

Pretty blase stuff for a 21-year-old who only a year earlier was pitching for USC, where baseball ranks far behind football, surfing, tanning, bikini-watching and numerous other sunny California pastimes.

Impressed, Wood welcomed his new rival for ace status on the Cubs by remarking, "He's a lot more prepared than I was to step right in."

Media Sandbags Sandberg

Ryne Sandberg's brilliance got plenty of appreciation from Cubs fans. It was well deserved. For 15 years, from 1982 through 1997, he was as consistent at bat and in the field as the Cubs were in the NL standings. He was mostly up; they were mostly down.

For me, at least, Ryno's success story provided one of the major puzzles in all my years of Chicago hoop, grid and diamond scribing. It seemed the longer he did his job with such understated efficiency, the less media appreciation he got. When another No. 23, a fellow by the name of Jordan, showed early every night before games in Chicago Stadium and later in the United Center to perfect his laser jumpers from every angle, his work ethic rated raves from writers, radio and TV.

Yet hours before every Cubs game, their No. 23 would be out there around his second base turf, taking grounder after grounder. His brilliant fielding was no accident—or error—though few seemed to notice.

"I have a routine before every game," Sandberg told me. "Grounders to my left and right, some double play pivots. Wrigley Field has high grass, so the ball gets through a lot faster in other parks, but you have to practice every day on cutting down the angle. I know what pitch is coming [because he can see the catcher's signs] and I know the hitters. I still have to work at it all the time."

This from a man who fielded his position better than anybody I've ever seen, with a major-league record of 123 straight errorless games, from June 21, 1989 to May 17, 1990, to prove it. Sandberg's range was astonishing, especially on shots up the middle. Old-time fans still talk about the play Jackie Robinson made against the Phillies to delay the Whiz Kids' 1950 pennant clinching, but Sandberg turned in such semi-miraculous stops so often that they seemed routine.

"Whatever Ryne hit was a bonus," said Harry Caray. "Everything a second baseman has to do, he was near the top in all of them. And he was the Cubs' leader by setting an example of coming to work every day, instead of the showboating and arm-waving you see now."

Yet when Sandberg signed a five-year contract worth over $30 million in 1992, the uproar drowned out the daily exploits of this latter-day Quiet Man. The wails of some Chicago columnists and electronic shouters was so loud, it sounded like they had to pay. Above and beyond that, with the emergence of charismatic Sammy Sosa and the presence of quotable Mark Grace, Sandberg's reluctance to hold court at his locker actually seemed to be resented by some of the media.

"He has no personality," was the most frequent grumble, even though Sandberg answered all questions and never stalked away from the postgame grilling in a huff, like some of his temperamental teammates (Danny Jackson, Scott Servais and Delino DeShields, to name a few) did when they had bad games.

When Sandberg retired abruptly in midseason, 1994, sat out a year, then came back to play two more seasons, he got bashed for both decisions. I still can't understand why, any more than the reasoning that led less than half of the eligible voters (he got only 49.2 percent) to agree this obvious Hall of Famer should make it in 2003, his first year of eligibility. Regardless, his 1996-1997 swan song produced 37 more homers, enough to become the all-time leader at second base with 277 (plus five more as a third baseman).

With the career totals he piled up at second base, Ryne Sandberg figures to make baseball's Hall of Fame soon. Cubs fans are disappointed that Ryno didn't get enough votes in 2003, his first try.

That, along with 2,386 hits—all except one as a Cub—
nine straight Gold Glove awards and a 1984 NL Most
Valuable Player Award should have put Ryno in the Hall of
Fame on the first ballot. Perhaps his Chicago media critics
insisted on a personality penalty, but Sandberg's career
numbers and consistency far outstrip such nitpicking
nonsense.

Grace Seldom Off Base

M ark Grace always knew the score and how to play
the game, on and off the field. That's what made
him a Chicago favorite for a dozen years as the Cubs' first
base fixture. When he opted for free agency, to finally get a
2001 World Series ring from the Arizona Diamondbacks, it
marked a turn-of-the-century farewell to all that.

Grace's Cubs lost more than they won, but he knew
how to make it more Graceful. Besides banging out more
base hits (1,754) than any other big-leaguer during the
1990s, he probably was the biggest clubhouse hit. Sammy
Sosa was the emerging superstar, but Grace was the one who
put things in perspective for the media.

Instead of those can-of-corn quotes ("That was a big
win for us"—any manager, or "We're busting our butts out
there"—any player), Grace almost always had something
interesting, and above all, quotable to fill notebook
scribblings and tape recorders in postgame postmortems.
Sosa got much better at it as his homer total mounted, but
not quite as glib and facile as Grace.

"I only hit one like that every couple of years, so I enjoyed watching it go," Grace said after launching a rare tape-measure Wrigley Field homer in 1993.

That was typical of Grace's knack for snappy repartee. The fancy-fielding first baseman knew when to play it straight, when to go in depth for earnest young would-be Red Smiths, when to kid around and when to be diplomatic about the Cubs' habit of coming up short, year after year. It was natural, almost inevitable, for friction to develop between him and Sosa, though both men were canny enough to keep it under wraps.

It was probably a little misunderstanding, Sosa said of the growing gap between his and Grace's lockers, which were at opposite ends of the clubhouse, both geographically and emotionally. "If Sammy's taking shots at me, I won't shoot back," Grace responded. "I thought we had a good relationship on the field."

Off the field? That's another story, although singles and doubles hitter Grace's career should not be defined by a spell of the petty jealousy almost all ballplayers get embroiled in. He was an outstanding first baseman, especially adept at scooping up shortstop Shawon Dunston's errant throws from the dirt, turning potential errors into outs and rescuing legions of grateful Cubs pitchers. Gracie won't get enough votes when he appears on the Hall of Fame ballot five years after retirement, but for Cubs fans, there is a highly unofficial, totally emotional Hall of Fame. It lives on in the Wrigley Field bleachers, and Grace belongs.

The Red Baron's a Real Gamer

Maybe the main reason for Cubs fans' love affair with Rick Sutcliffe was his abnormally high tolerance for pain. That's something they can relate to in the bleachers, the box seats and every other nook and Wrigley Field cranny, crammed with rooters smiling through their own wait-till-next-year misery.

A pitcher like Sutcliffe, going out to do battle inning after inning with a sore arm and little left on the ball except the cover, is their kind of guy. With all the teeth-gnashing, weeping and wailing when the Cubs blew that horrific 1984 NL playoff to the San Diego Padres, virtually nobody blamed the Red Baron. Sure, he went down in flames, letting a 3-0 lead evaporate in the fateful fifth game, but it was with all guns blazing. Sutcliffe's ailing shoulder throbbed by the time Cubs manager Jim Frey (too late) took him out during the Padres' game-winning rally.

What endeared the Red Baron to Cubs fans, besides his flaming beard, was the way he refused to blame anyone, other than himself, for the 1984 playoff calamity. He was not a finger-pointer or clubhouse lawyer, unlike some of his teammates. The search for scapegoats centered on Frey and first baseman Leon Durham, who committed a critical error in Game 5 at San Diego, shattering the dream of one more Wrigley Field World Series in the 20th century. Sutcliffe refused to take part in that witch hunt.

"Everybody else on the Cubs was as heartsick as I was when that series got away from us," the towering (six-foot, seven-inch) right-hander told me. "It was nobody's fault. Baseball can be a strange, humbling game."

Sutcliffe never stood taller than he did in the wake of that traumatic loss. His never-give-up attitude was to undergo even tougher tests in the years ahead. He took home a unanimous 1984 Cy Young Award for going 16-1 to spark the Cubs to their first-ever NL division crown, but arm trouble plagued him from then on. Despite pitching in pain, Rick barely missed a second Cy Young trophy in 1987, then became the first Cubs pitcher since Grover Cleveland Alexander (1925-26) to win consecutive home Opening Day starts in 1988-89.

Through it all, family man Sutcliffe kept his perspective and his sense of humor. Like most pitchers, he was superstitious. When arm woes multiplied during the '80s, he took to throwing away his spiked shoes after every game, wearing a new pair for the next start.

"I got to figuring they were bad luck," Sutcliffe said. "I finally figured out the problem was not in my feet. It's tough to win games when your shoulder hurts, your leg hurts and you can't throw hard."

The Hawk Flies High

In a narrow sense, Andre Dawson was a one-shot deal for the Cubs. The intense veteran, already hobbling on two sore knees, had to beg them to let him climb aboard their sinking ship in 1987.

The Cubs did so grudgingly, though only after a spring training circus that was highly entertaining for the fans, but demeaning to Dawson, a 10-year veteran, who offered a badly needed package of class, ability and results. Signing Dawson for $500,000, far below his market value, required a series of daily insult-trading screaming matches between Cubs general manager Dallas Green and agent Dick Moss.

Before long, The Hawk was whipping right field bleacherites into a frenzy that set the stage for Sammy Sosa's decade-plus of dominance on that same patch of Wrigley Field turf, still going strong into the 21st century.

Dawson didn't own the North Side for nearly that long, but he certainly did in 1987. The right-handed slugger had the kind of year Robert Redford never did in *The Natural*, slamming 27 of his 49 homers at home. He shared the home run crown with Oakland's Mark McGwire, but topped Sosa's future NL rival in other categories, especially fielding, to run away with National League MVP honors.

The list of Dawson's feats that year reads like a Babe Ruth biography. In a stretch that started with a game-winning grand slam on April 22, he piled up 131 RBIs in 140 games. Eight days later, he hit for the cycle against San Francisco and threw out the Giants' Roger Mason at first base after the startled batter thought he had singled to right. Twice, Hawk tomahawked five homers in a three-game stretch and drove Andre's Army into total delirium by whacking three out of Wrigley Field in consecutive turns at bat against the Phillies on Aug. 1.

No wonder the right field bleachers rose en masse to salute Dawson with bow-from-the-waist salaams when he hobbled out to his position. After a decade of virtual anonymity in Montreal, the taciturn outfielder, weary of the constant pain from a high-school football injury, was riding a wave of adulation.

"I never knew there were fans like that, anywhere," Dawson marveled.

Not one to wear emotion on his sleeve, Dawson let it all hang out on occasion, especially after Padres pitcher Eric Show, a notorious flake, bloodied the Hawk's lip with a high, hard fastball. Enraged, Dawson got up with fire in his eye and charged, chasing Show off the mound and into the visitors' dugout, while Wrigley fans roared gleefully. He showed a more compassionate side to me when I got a letter from a fan whose mother was terminally ill with cancer. She listened to games on a bedside radio, and Dawson was her hero. I took the letter to Hawk, who copied the lady's name on a baseball he autographed with a personal inscription.

A few months later, another letter asked me to convey the family's gratitude to Dawson.

"That baseball brightened my mother's last days," it said. "She died with it right next to the radio."

Dawson stuck around long enough to help the Cubs get into the 1989 NL playoffs. They lost, but he departed in 1993, still a winner.

Ernie's Place

He's still Mr. Cub, all these years later. The legend of Ernie Banks is the one thing that won't change as long as Wrigley Field stands where it is. I suppose that Clark and Addison will have to become a mega-mall or a 200-story condo or a home for aged and indigent aldermen one of these years, but I hope not in Ernie's lifetime—or mine.

I first met Ernie Banks around the Wrigley batting cage in 1970. Jack Brickhouse introduced me as a new guy on the Cubs beat. I don't recall the handshake banter that ensued, but I remember the smile that went with it. As long as he played there, Wrigley Field didn't need lights, because that smile lit up the park.

Banks was based in Los Angeles 15 years later, when I wrote my second book about the Cubs—*So You Think You're a Die-Hard Cub Fan*, but that cheerful smile came right through the phone when he agreed to do the foreword. Very few people have his ability to see the best in everything and everybody, without sounding like a used car salesman. What he sells is sunshine, fun and Wrigley Field, all wrapped up in the title he gave to his ballpark—the Friendly Confines.

That's not all Ernie contributed, through good times and bad for the Cubs. He never got to the World Series everybody thought was coming in 1969 to cap his magnificent career. Definitely unfair, but so is baseball at times, because it's so much like life. The good guys don't always win, and Banks is exhibit A in that category.

Still, 512 homers, a Hall of Fame berth, 19 years as the Cubs' shortstop, first baseman and chief cheerleader, plus his personal No. 14 flag, flapping in the breeze above Wrigley Field's left field foul pole, compensate for that one missing link to complete the chain of a wonderful life in baseball. In truth, *It's a Wonderful Life* should be the title of a movie starring Ernie, not Jimmy Stewart. Although Banks endured his share of the shabby treatment routinely meted out to black players in his younger days with the Kansas City Monarchs, it couldn't dent his spirit. Neither did scrawled death threats from hateful morons to Banks, Hank Aaron and other black stars following the trail blazed by Jackie Robinson.

That's why it was fun to be around Ernie. He enjoyed, life, people, baseball, and good times. I really enjoyed writing about the Wrigley Field festivities on May 30, 1970, honoring Banks and Billy Williams between games of a doubleheader. Colleague Dick Dozer of the *Tribune* gave Ernie a bronzed sports page trumpeting his 500th homer on May 12. My dressing room story was on that page, and one of my most prized souvenirs is a T-shirt reproduction of it. Before or since, I never wore one of my bylines on my chest, but in this case, I'm happy to make an exception.

Even more than his feats on the field, though, Banks's memory endures because he's a rallying point for Cubs fans. When Harry Caray lauded fun at the old ballpark, he agreed that Ernie's legacy was the source.

"Opening Day [at Wrigley Field, of course] should be a national holiday," Banks trumpeted.

None of the 2,793 Wrigley Field customers thought a legend was in the making when the skinny shortstop started his first Cubs game on Sept. 17, 1953, at the tail end of another losing (65-89) season. The Cubs got edged out by the Phillies, 16-4, and Banks went hitless, but that didn't last long. It seemed like the blink of an eye—and 499 home runs—later that 39-year-old Mr. Cub disappointed a 1970 Mother's Day throng of 32,255 by just missing that historic 500th. It came two days later, but that sunny afternoon would have been the perfect time in the Friendly Confines.

It might have been, it could have been, but it wasn't. Banks lined a vicious shot into the left field vines off Reds fireballer Wayne Simpson (who had vowed "Banks won't hit No. 500 off me"). He was right, only because Ol' Ern's sore knees made him stop at third, while the ball ricocheted wildly.

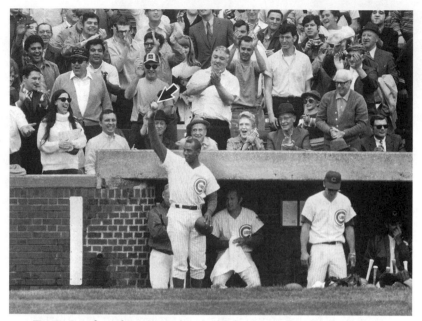

Ernie Banks salutes Wrigley Field fans, waving the ball he just drove into the bleachers for career home run No. 500. It's a new century now, but Ernie's still the people's choice.

"I need more speed," he chuckled. "I thought about going for an inside-the-park homer, but between second and third, I felt like I had a piano on my back."

Anyway, Ernie carried the Cubs on his back for almost two decades.

Sweet Swinger's Reward

There's always one mope who can't help raining on a sunny parade. In this case, it was a journeyman player named Wally Moon, whose specialty was lofting pop-fly homers over the screen the Dodgers erected in their makeshift Coliseum ballpark when they first moved to Los Angeles in 1958. He'd have to buy a ticket to get into the Hall of Fame, but got miffed when Billy Williams was voted in.

"They've watered down some of the criteria," Moon moaned. "Williams hit .290, but others hit .330. The Hall should be a very exclusive club."

He was a very small minority, drowned out by the tidal wave of congratulations when the Sweet Swinger took his rightful place among baseball's immortals, class of 1987. Williams was among the classiest of big-leaguers for all of his 18 seasons, 16 with the Cubs. He proved it again with an emotional speech when his plaque went up in Cooperstown .

"I wouldn't be here without Shirley," he said of his wife, who sobbed through the ceremony, with their four daughters. Billy also took quiet pride in his then-NL record streak of 1,117 consecutive games. I covered the streak-breaking game on Sept. 3, 1970, watching Billy handle it with his innate dignity.

When Williams was swinging a hot bat, pitchers quaked. Line drives seemed to explode off his bat in those stretches, like July 11, 1972, with eight for eight in a doubleheader against Houston and April 9, 1969, when he became only the 28th player in history to collect four doubles in a game.

"Doubles for Abner Doubleday," Williams cracked.

Fergie's Fine

Ferguson Jenkins played baseball the same way fellow Canadian Gordie Howe played hockey. No nonsense, all business, eye on the ball—or the puck. If anybody got in the way of either man, he was likely to be knocked down, with a brushback pitch or a cross-check.

Jenkins was a fan favorite because he was the Cubs' ace for most of his eight Chicago seasons, the stopper they depended on to snap losing streaks. The strapping right-hander seldom got the headlines he deserved, despite six straight 20-victory seasons, from 1967 through 1972, a feat matched by just one other Cubs pitcher, Mordecai "Three-Finger" Brown (1906-11). I dubbed him the "Unknown Winner," and Fergie agreed.

"I don't know why I don't get the same national publicity as Tom Seaver and Vida Blue," he told me. "The first time I won 20, they said I was lucky. I kept doing it, and they didn't say anything."

A 1980 drug bust cast a shadow over Jenkins's Hall of Fame prospects, but his 284-236 career record, along with 49 shutouts and 3,192 strikeouts provided his passport. He joined Banks and Williams from the 1969 Cubs, adding a known winner to the talented team that couldn't win, for unknown reasons.

"Fergie made it look easy," said his Cub catcher, Randy Hundley. "He just went out there, took the ball and threw it past the hitters."

CHAPTER 5

GOING OUT OF THEIR MASTERMINDS

A lot of ex-Cubs managers probably would agree with the chicken thief who got tarred and feathered and ridden out of town on a rail. When asked for his reaction to the ordeal, the miscreant replied, "If it wasn't for the honor of the thing, I'd just as soon walk."

Well, manager after manager has taken that one-way walk, a treadmill to oblivion from the Cubs' dugout to the unemployment compensation office, since I wandered onto the baseball beat a year after the colossal calamity of 1969. Leo Durocher was the dugout dictator then, alternately charming, haranguing and finally infuriating the Cubs into contending status. But he couldn't get them over the hump and into the playoffs, so Leo had to go, opening the floodgates for a tidal wave of managerial impersonators.

Dusty Baker, one of the few who looked like the genuine article, became the 20th Cubs manager since Durocher. Sometimes as many a three in the same season spun in and out of that revolving door with dizzying, dismaying rapidity. That wasn't quite as ridiculous as owner P. K. Wrigley's brainstorm, the College of Coaches, featuring a hilarious five-way backstabbing tournament in 1961-62, although just as futile. Jim Riggleman (1995-99) was the only field boss who lasted for five years in the odd Cubs' odyssey from Durocher to Dusty.

If I ranked Cubs managers by listing the characters at the top, Durocher would be the leadoff bench brainstormer, followed by Herman Franks, Lee Elia and Jim Essian. I have too much respect for Don Zimmer to call him a character, except in the most affectionate sense, because he has real character, besides being a walking baseball museum and treasure chest of diamond lore. So, starting with the new kid on the block, here's a look at all those would-be Casey Stengels.

Dusty Road to Wrigley

Mike Remlinger tried to be a prophet while profiting from the Cubs. When he signed a three-year, $11 million contract to switch bullpens, from Atlanta to Chicago, the lefty reliever predicted, "Dusty Baker will give the Cubs the credibility they needed. Spend a few minutes with him, and you feel at ease."

What the Cubs really needed from their new manager, of course, was an incredible leap to the top of the NL Central Division standings. Before leaving the Golden Gate Bridge behind to work for a team that's had fans jumping off the Michigan Avenue Bridge for a half-century, Baker got assurances that the Tribune Company's deep pockets would cough up cold cash to lure new talent for 2003.

Sure enough, Dusty hadn't even dusted off his clubhouse desk when Cubs general manager Jim Hendry plunged into a frantic flurry of roster roulette. With all those new faces to plug in around superstar Sammy Sosa and a promising array of starting pitchers, expectations were high for the former San Francisco skipper. Perhaps for the first time since Durocher departed in 1972, Cubs fans felt that Baker could take them to where he couldn't quite get the Giants—a World Series victory.

"Why not us?" Baker asked when he took the reins soon after the Cubs concluded their 2002 orgy of self-flagellation under fired Don Baylor and the interim innocent bystander, Bruce Kimm.

Naturally, the Cubs pounced on that as their new marketing tool. It worked for the White Sox (remember "The Kids Can Play"?), but Cubs fans won't really be happy unless their next T-shirt reads "One More in '04". That puts added pressure on Baker to make it happen overnight. If he does, Chicago will erupt like Mt. Vesuvius, erasing a bear market of frustration from the Bears' nosedive.

Baker roamed the outfield for 19 years with the Braves, Dodgers, Giants and Oakland A's, hitting a solid .278 with 242 homers and a growing reputation as a manager on the field. Understandably, the California native needed only a short apprenticeship as a Giants coach before starting a decade as their manager in 1993. Like the rest of the Giants, he was mentally measuring himself for a World Series ring before the Anaheim Angels rallied to win Game 6 and snatch the prize away in the winner-take-all finale.

Dusty Baker. Photo courtesy of the Chicago Cubs.

"We got to the doorstep, but they [the Angels] slammed it in our faces," Baker said with a resigned shrug.

Undeterred, the Cubs blew the dust off their purse strings to enrich Dusty by $15 million over the next four years. If he wins, it could be a lot longer. If not, the 53-year-old Baker won't age gracefully in the Friendly Confines.

Leo, You Ain't Lion

In 1966, Leo Durocher came to Chicago, touted as the savior of the sagging Cubs franchise. Fans with long memories saw some irony when the same role was thrust on Dusty Baker more than three decades later. Actually, comparing these two Cubs managers is an exercise in apples-and-oranges futility.

It's more than just that Baker is a California guy, bringing his laid-back image to Chicago, or that Durocher was a New York guy, wrapping up every abrasive Big Apple stereotype in his stylishly dressed, flamboyant lifestyle. After all, Leo ended up in Palm Springs, hanging out with such transplanted Easterners as Frank Sinatra.

And Baker, in almost three decades of baseball travel, along with playing for ultra-competitive Dodgers manager Tommy Lasorda, quickly learned that the meek do not inherit first place.

Still, Durocher was unique, in or out of baseball. Maybe the most self-centered man I ever met, he knew how to play the role, changing personalities in the blink of an eye to deal with any situation. I've seen him charm the pants off banquet audiences, lowering that rasping voice to make even the drunks at the back tables believe they were being taken into his confidence.

"Why, gentlemen," Durocher would purr. "You wouldn't believe these umpires nowadays. There's nobody like Jocko Conlan today. The way Jocko and I got into it, chest to chest..."

And Leo was off and running, reinventing for the 1,000th time his famous shin-kicking duel with Conlan. Each version was different, but they all ended up with the same punch (or rather, kick) line: "I got hurt a lot worse, because Jocko was wearing shinguards and steel toe plates, kicking my ankles. I only had baseball socks on."

It always brought down the house. Leo knew they were waiting for his most famous line, "Nice guys finish last," so he saved it for last, denying he ever said it without actually denying it. This man was much too smart to disown the misquote that earned him immortality of sorts in Bartlett's Quotations. What Leo actually did in his Brooklyn Dodger managing days was point to the New York Giants' dugout and say, "Lot of nice guys over there, but they're in last place."

But that was Durocher all over, adapting whatever happened to suit his purposes. He reveled in the labels hung on him by sportswriters ("Lippy Leo" or "Leo the Lion" or "The Little Shepherd of Coogan's Bluff" or whatever), rewarding them with choice quotes from his bottomless pit of baseball savvy. Yes, he was a great manager for 24 years, with an overall 2,008-1,731 record (535-526 as Cubs skipper), and I stand by the column I wrote years ago, outlining the reasons why Durocher belonged in the Hall of Fame.

He finally got there in 1994, years later than he should have.

Why? Because there was a dark side to this complex man. Leo made so many enemies and piled up so much emotional baggage over the years that it's a wonder he got in at all. Some purists still point to Durocher's shady connections and backroom dealings with gamblers, hoodlums and assorted lowlifes that got him suspended from baseball for the 1947 season "for activities detrimental to baseball."

In his stormy six-plus years on the Chicago scene (1966-72), Durocher's penchant for alienating people played a major part in his downfall. Case in point: Cubs broadcaster Jack Brickhouse, eventually turning from a Leo booster to a Leo basher. When I sat down with Brickhouse to tape some memories for a previous book, he fed me lots of insight on the unraveling of Durocher's Cubs.

"Getting his facts straight never was a priority for Leo," Jack told me. "He gradually lost that razor-sharp instinct for managing and took the team down with him."

The ball was still very much in Leo's court when I arrived on the Cubs scene in 1970. I believe that team was even better than the failed Cubs of '69, but it again finished in second place. Durocher gave me the once-over when I first walked into his clubhouse office. He had a knack for gravitating to the most important people in any crowd. I wasn't important, but the *Chicago Tribune* was, so he knew he had to deal with me.

I couldn't figure out why Leo once raised his voice, to make sure I overheard him, while ostentatiously phoning to order roses for his wife, Lynn Walker Goldblatt, a Chicago TV personality. After a while, I began to understand that impressing the peasants was just part of his lifelong ego trip. Anyway, two and a half years of covering Leo, the increasingly

Leo Durocher (2, back to camera) greets his up-and-coming Cubs in Wrigley Field. Leo the Lip had them on the verge of the 1969 playoffs, but it was all downhill for him after that late-season fadeout.

toothless Lion, was a fascinating, spicy bowl of my Chicago sports stew.

Nice Guy Finishes First—Once

The poster boy for all the nice guys in baseball was— and doubtless still is—Jim Riggleman. In his five seasons of struggling to nudge the Cubs into the postseason picture, I don't recall Rigs raising his voice in anger more than once or twice, despite unlimited opportunities to do so. Maybe that was his fatal flaw.

Or perhaps not. It's entirely possible that a reincarnation of Connie Mack, John McGraw and Casey Stengel couldn't have manged the Cubs of 1995-99 into the playoffs more than once. The one time they got there—in 1998—was a quintessential Cubs moment. They trudged off the field in Houston on Sept. 27, believing a last-game loss to the Astros had ended their season. Instead, the Cubs backed into a wild-card tie with the Giants, then beat them in a one-game playoff for the right to get swept out, 3-0, of their playoff with the Atlanta Braves.

'Twas ever thus for the Cubs, at least since 1945. Riggleman, liked and respected by his players and the media, was a good manager for the Cubs, but like a lot of bad managers who preceded him, he was unable to break their cycle of one good season, three or four or more bad seasons. His frustration couldn't be contained in 1999, when Cubs contenders became pretenders with startling swiftness.

Sitting pretty at 32-23 on June 8, they folded like wet Kleenex, plummeting to 30 games under .500 at the end, on the wings of an 8-24 August record.

Naturally, Riggleman had to take the fall for his players' shoddy performance. He saw it coming midway through the season and tried, too late, to stop the bleeding.

"The rats are the first ones to jump off a sinking ship," Rigs said. "We'll find out who the rats are."

The other major Riggleman meltdown was a dugout shouting match with Sammy Sosa in 1997, when the slugger ignored a sign, ran on his own and got cut down trying to steal second base. Tempers already were frayed by a horrendous 0-14 start that season, the worst losing streak in Cubs history.

"Sammy wasn't supposed to run, but he did anyway," the miffed manager said. "I had to talk to him in front of the club or the other players would have lost respect for me. I want everybody, not just Sammy, to play for the team."

Predictably, soon after the 1999 debacle, the rats were still cashing paychecks, but Riggleman wasn't.

Seasoned in the ups and downs of the game, he took it in stride. The Cubs had a fatal hole in their rotation during his final season at the helm, because Kerry Wood, '98 NL Rookie of the Year, missed it all to recover from elbow surgery. So Jon Lieber, at 10-11, was their only double-digit winner. Rather than get Riggleman fresh talent, his bosses elected to make him walk the plank. Characteristically, he took it in stride.

"Maybe I should have agreed about some [players'] shortcomings, instead of defending them over and over," Rigs reflected.

Baylor's Jail

Perhaps pondering Riggleman's fate before he came aboard as manager in 2000, Don Baylor decided that the Cubs needed two things—one: discipline, and two: a different attitude. Before Baylor got fired, midway through his third season, there was an attitude change—from bad to worse.

As for discipline, most of that got inflicted on the media covering the Cubs. Sammy Sosa's terrific home run duels with the Cards' Mark McGwire, on top of the Cubs' rare playoff appearance in 1998, intensified the pre- and postgame crush of writers, radio and TV people, clamoring to shower free publicity on the team owned by a mammoth communications empire.

For Riggleman, it was no problem, because that gabby guy gladly would talk your ear off, one-on-one or the whole media mob on him. It soon became clear that access to Baylor would be much more severely limited. Only the media biggies were allowed in the manager's office, upstairs in the new home clubhouse under the left-field stands. That cozy hideaway, where I'd spent hours yakking about this and that, sometimes even baseball, with Don Zimmer, Jim Lefebvre, Riggleman and other Cubs managers, now was off limits.

But the move that stuck in almost everybody's craw was cramming the postgame media sessions into a tiny cubicle next to the umpires' dressing room. Baylor and requested players took turns squeezing behind a roped-off desk, often encircled by a ring of TV cameras that made it difficult for the ink-stained wretches in the rear to see or hear what was going on. My old *Chicago Tribune* sports editor, Cooper Rollow, used to caution us beat guys, "Don't expect sympathy from the fans when you gripe about your working conditions. Lots of them would kill to have your job."

Coop was right. Kiddingly, I dubbed the Cubs' cramped postgame penalty box "Stalag 25," a pointed reference to Baylor's uniform number, but other media people beefed less good-humoredly, including visiting writers. Regardless, the real focus on the Baylor regime was, as it should have been, on the Cubs' performance. With occasional exceptions, the new manager's honeymoon with Chicago's media and fans lasted through his mostly dismal 65-97 inaugural in 2000, because they wanted both him and the Cubs to succeed.

"Our fans expect us to lose," he told me early in that season, taking a look at Wrigley Field's rapidly filling seats, although gametime was hours away. "They come out here to enjoy this ballpark. I want them to start enjoying watching the Cubs win."

In 2001, they did, albeit briefly. The Cubs ripped off a 12-game victory streak (May 19-June 2), their longest run of total success in 66 years, only to become the Cubs again—and as usual—down the stretch.

Injuries added to the frustration, so Baylor couldn't even make it past the 2002 All-Star break. Both he and the Cubs were out of it by then, so the axe fell on July 5, with ex-Cub and White Sox catcher Bruce Kimm coming in from Iowa to rearrange the deck chairs on the sinking S.S. Cubtanic.

"The talent on the field does not equal the victory total," was Cubs president Andy MacPhail's terse see-you-later message, resigned to paying Baylor another $1.3 million for not managing the Cubs in 2003.

Trebelhorn's In Trouble

King Louis XVI accurately predicted the bloodshed of the coming French Revolution when he proclaimed: "After me, the deluge." Emperor Leo the First might well have foreseen the same gory future for the Cubs when Durocher went to the guillotine (figuratively speaking, of course) in 1972.

With few exceptions, the parade of fruitless, and mostly clueless, pretenders to the Cubs' managerial throne has continued in an unbroken shuffle since then. Tom Trebelhorn was one of them in the strike-shortened 1994 season, his lone turn at the helm, with few noticing his arrival or departure. This could have been one of the most forgettable Wrigley Field campaigns of all time, and that's saying a lot.

In fairness to the former Milwaukee Braves pilot, his opening day pitcher was lonesome traveler Mike Morgan, making the first of two brief sojourns on the Cubs' roster during his lucrative 12-team tour of both leagues. Perhaps arm-weary from toting suitcases from town to town, the right-hander spent much of that season on the disabled list, in between compiling a 2-10 record and a 6.69 ERA. Rookie Steve Trachsel was the staff ace, so to speak, with a 9-7 record, but Willie—no, not Ernie—Banks made 23 starts, more than any other Cubs pitcher. No wonder Trebelhorn was reduced to responses like this when asked, during another of the '94 Cubs' frequent tailspins, if losing bothered his players:

"Of course," he sputtered. "They're human, just like anybody else."

No Pennant Fever for Lefebvre

Jim Lefebvre was bitterly disappointed when he didn't get rehired after managing the Cubs to a rare glimpse of break-even territory at 162-162 overall in 1992-93. The longtime Dodger second baseman was a fierce competitor and a solid baseball man. He just couldn't get on the same page with Cubs (and ex-White Sox) general manager Larry Himes, who ruffled feathers wherever he went.

So Lefebvre lost that power struggle, although Himes got handed his own bus ticket after the Trebelhorn debacle of 1994. The cycle of inept Cubs management, continually hiring managers who couldn't get the job done because their teams were not stocked with multimillionaire free agents, continued right up to 2003, when Dusty Baker made signing some high-priced talent a condition of his leaving the Giants to manage the Cubs.

Grade A for Z-Ball

The Cubs should have kept Don Zimmer, moved him into the front office, paid for titanium replacements of his chronically sore knees and given him enough money to stock the roster with guys who would run through ivy-covered brick walls to catch fly balls. In the end, all Zim got was the gate.

He left behind a legacy of one NL Eastern Division crown in 1989, followed by an excruciating NL pennant playoff loss to the Giants, when the Cubs unaccountably left their hearts in San Francisco, along with an awful lot of high-energy, high-risk, highly entertaining baseball.

Zim was a riverboat gambler at heart. He had the Cubs doing things they haven't done before or since, especially on the bases. The 1989 bunch did things under Zimmer's fiery prodding that almost all teams did back in the dead-ball era—bunt, squeeze, steal, hit-and-run, run-and-hit, even the lost art of hitting behind the runner. Listening to Zimmer talk about how baseball should be played was even more fun than watching the Cubs try to play it his way.

"A lot of these kids get rushed up to the majors now before they've seen a lot of fundamentals," Zimmer told me during one of those relaxed bull sessions in his clubhouse office. "Let's be realistic. If you got a million-dollar bonus just to sign a contract right out of high school, would you want to go down to the minors and listen to some bald-headed old coach tell you how to play the game?"

If that bald guy happened to be Zimmer, young players willing to listen could get a priceless free education. Zimmer had seen and done it all through his eventful half-century as a player, manager and coach in the minors and majors. The scrappy infielder paid his dues along the way, as evidenced by a silver plate in his head to mark the spot of a near-fatal beaning.

When Zim was in an expansive mood, he'd talk about the most bitter defeat of them all. That was the 1978 American League pennant playoff in Fenway Park, when he managed the Boston Red Sox. They lost it to the Yankees on ex-White Sox shortstop Bucky Dent's three-run homer, lofted over the left field Green Monster..

"When Bucky hit the ball, I thought it was a pop fly," Zimmer related, with a sad shake of his head. "It just kept carrying."

The Red Sox are the only other big-league team capable of matching Cubs fans' tales of woe at a might-have-been meeting on Heartbreak Hill. The Beantown Brigade hasn't won a World Series since 1918, a decade after the Cubs captured their last one. So Zimmer knew what he was up against in Wrigley Field, where he played for manager Lou Boudreau in 1960 and for the infamous Cubs' revolving College of Coaches in 1961.

Despite his hobbled knees, advancing age and assorted ailments, Zimmer's zest for battle never dimmed.

As Cubs manager (1988-91) or on their coaching staff (1984-86), whenever tempers flared and benches emptied for brawls, Zim led the charge and leaped into the fray. He wrenched his neck in a 1984 battle royale with the archrival Mets, but earned respect from the players, bringing them together for a drive that ended the Cubs' 39-year absence from the postseason picture. A Met pitcher named Ed Lynch touched off the fisticuffs by throwing at Cubs batter Keith "Zonk" Moreland.

Ironically, a decade later, it was that same Lynch who began a six-year stint with the Cubs as their general manager. In sharp contrast with Zimmer's bottomless reservoir of how-to-do-it-right baseball in their employ, his Tribune Co. bosses chose to get rid of him. He's still bitter about that, especially the final kiss-off.

"Guys in Italian silk suits who knew nothing about baseball were telling me I wasn't doing the job," he said.

For Zimmer, at least, things turned out right. Yankees manager Joe Torre, a league leader in class and savvy, brought Zim in to be his bench coach. The results of firing Zimmer in Chicago and hiring him in New York can be gauged simply by comparing the Yankees' yearly spot atop the AL standings against the Cubs' customary lease on the NL basement.

The Essian Experiment

When Don Zimmer departed after the Cubs got off to an 18-20 start in 1991, the Cubs went to the other extreme, bringing in a man with no big-league managing experience. He was former White Sox catcher Jim Essian, summoned from the Cubs' Iowa farm team on May 22.

Even Cubs fans, accustomed to seeing unlikely suspects posing as their team's manager, were perplexed by this move. Essian, the 40-year-old freshman, astonished them even more by winning his first three games.

"That man is a genius," gushed Cubs outfielder Dwight Smith, whose objectivity might have been slightly tarnished by the fact that Essian started him in left field, replacing George Bell, who got traded a year later to the White Sox for Sammy Sosa.

Essian, a yoga devotee, brought in former Sox teammate Richie Zisk as the hitting instructor. They'd been together on the fondly remembered 1977 South Side Hit Men, who packed Comiskey Park that summer for Bill Veeck's rent-a-player 198-homer derby, featuring Zisk ("Pitch at Risk to Richie Zisk") and ex-Cub Oscar Gamble. Unfortunately, Zisk couldn't get either team into the playoffs, sealing Essian's fate as a one-shot pilot for the Cubs.

"Stick" the Wrong Pick

The Cubs' managerial circus hit a new high, or perhaps low, in 1986, when Dallas Green thumbed through a directory of big-league executives, searching for a successor to manager Jim Frey. Green's self-styled "New Tradition" for the Cubs crumbled when he came up with the wrong name.

It was Gene "Stick" Michael, an ex-Yankee shortstop who stuck around in their front office to cope as best he could with volcanic eruptions from the powerful ego of "The Boss," George Steinbrenner, a force to be reckoned with, both in baseball and New York cafe society. Michael managed the Cubs through the last half of 1986 and yet another losing season in '87, then went back to New York, leaving no noticeable trace of his short stay.

"It was hard to tell whether Stick or John Vukovich [Cubs bench coach] really ran the team," a baffled player opined.

Another entry in the It Fugures department quickly followed for the rudderless Cubs organization.

Green quit abruptly—or was he pushed?—right after the 1987 debacle, heading back East for (surprise) a couple of contentious, unproductive managerial tours with both the Yankees and Mets. In his place, the Cubs installed— who else?—Jim Frey, the Cubs manager Green had hired and fired.

Frey Not?

Jim Frey's tenure in the Cub dugout was a smashing success in 1984. The Cubs turned on this toddlin' town by barging to the doorstep of their first World Series since 1945, but got no closer. The trauma of losing three straight playoff games in San Diego, when all the Cubs needed to wrap up the NL pennant was to play at their customary .333 road pace, hung over the team like an epidemic of swine flu.

True, the constant arm and shoulder miseries of Cubs ace Rick Sutcliffe played a major role in their downfall. Nothing much else worked, either, so the bottom dropped out in 1985 and another managerial troika of Frey, John Vukovich and Gene Michael couldn't stop the bleeding a year later. Oh, well, the Roar of '84 sure was fun while it lasted.

We Feel for Ya, Elia

L ee Elia was one of the finest all-around athletes ever
to come out of the Philadelphia area. When I was a
young cub (reporter, not player) at the *Philadelphia Inquirer,*
his feats in football, basketball, baseball and track made the
paper almost daily. Elia chose to become a baseball lifer,
playing briefly for the 1966 White Sox (80 games, .206
batting average) and the 1968 Cubs (15 games, .176 average)
before turning to managing in the minors.

Eddie Stanky [Sox manager] was about to cut me in
spring training," Elia recalled. "Then I hit a pinch-hit grand
slam off Bob Gibson, so they let me go north with the team."

When Elia came back to Chicago 14 years later with
some impressive coaching and managing credentials, Cubs
fans were willing to take a wait-and-see-attitude on the
newcomer. After all, he had been manager Dallas Green's
third base coach with the Phillies, the team that knocked
off the favored Kansas City Royals in the 1980 World Series.
Elia looked, walked and talked like a young man (only 44)
with leadership skills, ready to grow as a manager. It didn't
take long for that rosy scenario—and Elia himself—to go
down in flames.

"Dallas and I look at things the same way," Elia said
before taking the reins in 1982. "He's tough, and if he's
losing the argument, he just yells louder."

Those words proved prophetic on April 29, 1983, just
after reliever Lee Smith's wild pitch cost the Cubs a 4-3 loss
to the Dodgers. Enraged because his players got heckled by
the sparse Wrigley Field crowd, Elia blew up like a runaway
rocket, spewing profane venom over Cubs fans.

Manager Lee Elia can't believe what he's hearing from umpire John McSherry in this 1983 debate. Box-seat fans tune in eagerly, but pitching coach Billy Connors (right) feigns disinterest.

"If they're the real Cub fans, they can kiss my ass," Elia said in one of his milder references to Wrigley customers during a lengthy, emotional tirade. It almost got him fired on the spot when general manager Green heard the tape made by veteran Chicago sportscaster Les Grobstein.

As things turned out, Elia's quick, profuse apology earned him only a stay of execution. He was gone before the 1983 season ground to a merciful 71-91 halt, with interim manager Charlie Fox at the helm. Basically a nice guy, Elia coached elsewhere and mended fences on every trip to Chicago.

From Hot Dogs to Franks

If they ever want to make a TV sitcom about baseball, blending humor with reality, the Chicago Cubs would be the role-model team, with a manager who looks and acts a lot like Herman Franks.

Herman was definitely not your stereotype skipper, the crusty old coot with the heart of gold, like the ones in *Damn Yankees* or the Bob Uecker movies. Not that he was mean and dumb; far from it. Franks had a mean streak, but he knew a lot about baseball and business, enjoying far more success in the latter field. A millionaire investor, he struck out as Cubs manager (1977-79) and later as their general manager (1981).

On a 1978 Cubs trip to San Diego, Franks took some writers, including myself, for a stroll near the world-famous Del Coronado Hotel. Pointing to a row of luxury apartment houses farther down the beach, he said, "Those are mine."

The Cubs did make a pretty good run at the top in 1977, Herman's dugout debut. The familiar late-fade scenario removed the rosy glow of optimism, and Franks had to settle for entertaining the fans during the rest of his tenure by staging running feuds with Jose Cardenal, Bill Buckner and assorted media critics. It was a fun time to be on the Cubs beat, with every day providing new grist for the comedy mill. Through it all, the rotund manager held court every day in the dugout or his office, spraying tobacco juice with equal-opportunity zest on his shoes and those of bystanders.

Herman didn't need the money or the job, and he certainly didn't need the media. Sometimes he just liked to have us around while he alternately talked and munched his postgame beef sandwich, dripping gravy on his undershirt. Any conclusions we drew about the Cubs' performance, he made it clear, were strictly up to us.

"You saw it—you write it," was the customary response when asked for his insights. This was not a man who dwelt on history, tradition or Sparky Anderson-style diamond lore. I knew Franks had broken into the majors as a catcher with the Philadelphia A's, so I asked him what it was like to play for legendary manager Connie Mack, also a catcher back in the 19th century.

"How would I know?" he replied. "Who gives a damn about that?"

That was Herman all over—a big barrel of laughs.

Motley Cub Crew

Lots of other managers came and went during my three-plus decades of trying to figure out, mostly in vain, what the heck the Cubs were up to now. Some were mere blips on the radar screen, like Preston Gomez (1980), Frank Lucchesi (1987), Joe Altobelli (1991) and Bruce Kimm (2002). Even such a respected baseball figure as Whitey Lockman (1972-74), who picked up the baton dropped by Leo Durocher, couldn't turn the Cubs around.

For my money, the runners-up to Don Zimmer and Jim Riggleman in the good guy category were Jim Marshall (1974-76) and Joe Amalfitano (1979-81). Marshall tried to stretch a thin staff by yanking his pitchers quicker than most managers, so I dubbed him "Captain Hook."

That winter, I got a Christmas card from Marshall. It was signed, "Captain Hook." Anyone capable of managing the Cubs and keeping his sense of humor gets my vote.

CHAPTER 6

THE WALLS
OF IVY

Wrigley Field belongs to a lot more people than just Tribune Company stockholders.

This one-and-only baseball park, seemingly frozen in time, is more than just a slice of Chicago history, too. It's a symbol of what James Earl Jones described in that famous movie as "What baseball should be, and could be . . ." In short, it's America's field of dreams.

Only one other ballpark can rival Wrigley, both in longevity and loveability. That's Boston's Fenway Park, which opened for business in 1912, two years after the original Comiskey Park, on Chicago's South Side. But in 1914, another park went up at Clark and Addison Streets on the North Side at a cost of $250,000, heavy money for those days.

It was Weeghman Park, built to house the Chicago Whales of the short-lived Federal League. Not much of a team, as things turned out, but a whale of a baseball shrine.

Soon known as Cubs Park, when that charter NL franchise moved there in 1916, it became Wrigley Field in 1926, because the gum company's family had bought out owner "Lucky Charlie" Weeghman in 1919.

Before long, everybody knew the name and fame of a place where new chapters of diamond lore were added yearly. The incredible double no-hit duel between Jim "Hippo" Vaughn of the Cubs and Cincinnati's Fred Toney on May 2, 1917, served as a warning that the home team was fated to suffer many such heartbreaking moments in decades to come. Vaughn lost his no-no and the game, 1-0, in the 10th inning

Even Wrigley Field's all-time moment piled more misery on Cubs fans. It was Babe Ruth's called-shot home run off the Cubs' Charlie Root in Game 3 of the World Series, on Oct. 1, 1932. The Bambino allegedly pointed to the center field bleachers before depositing Root's next delivery there, setting up a Series sweep for the Yankees, along with one of baseball's most durable controversies. Root denied to his dying day that Ruth had called his shot, but I don't believe him.

Why? Because Pat Pieper, the Wrigley Field public address announcer, had been moved upstairs, over his loud protest, from the field to the press box when I started covering the Cubs in 1970. Pieper was a living witness to Wrigley history from the day the Cubs moved in until he retired in 1974. For years, he walked around the field, from first base to third, shouting that day's batteries through a megaphone. Later, generations of Cubs fans grew up savoring Pieper's stentorian tones on the field mike: "Tenshun! Tenshun, please! Have your pencils and scorecards ready and I'll give you the correct lineups for today's game..."

If Pat Pieper said something happened at Wrigley Field, I'm convinced that it did happen. So one day I asked him about it in the lull between batting practice and the game's start. He'd been grilled about the Ruth-Root dispute many times, but the grand old man of Wrigley Field never tired of talking about it.

"Absolutely, the Babe pointed to the center field bleachers," Pieper told me. "I was sitting a few feet away from him [on his familiar three-legged stool, perched against the low grandstand wall to the right of home plate], and there was no mistaking where he pointed. He was telling Root where his next pitch would go, and that's exactly where it went. Ruth called his shot."

That majestic gesture overshadowed the most famous Wrigley home run by a Cub. Gabby Hartnett's "Homer in the Gloaming," off Pittsburgh's Mace Brown on Sept. 28, 1938, wrapped up the NL pennant for the Cubs, boring through the gathering darkness to land in the left field bleachers. Ernie Banks launched his 500th career home run into those same seats 32 years later. In between, Stan Musial got his 3,000th hit and Pete Rose tied Ty Cobb's big-league record with his 4,191st hit, both in Wrigley Field.

Sammy Sosa's prodigious home runs provide plenty of present-day thrills. And the pitching performances keep piling up. Kerry Wood's 20-strikeout magnificence against Houston on May 6, 1998, might not be matched in the remainder of Wrigley's legendary lifetime—but don't bet on it. Despite the frigid temperatures of April, the fickle winds and blinding sun of every part of every season and the constant uproar about proposed alterations, the Friendly Confines endure, just too beloved to die. While Fenway Park belongs to all of New England, Wrigley Field belongs to all of America.

Back in the 1930s, the Great Depression gripped America, but things were more cheerful around Wrigley Field. Cubs fans flock for tickets to the 1935 World Series, though the Detroit Tigers beat their team in six games.

No ballpark I've ever seen generates the kind of emotion I've been hearing about Wrigley Field for over three decades. Overwhelmingly, it's favorable, much more so from the fans than the players. Some of the notes and quotes I've gathered over the years follow.

Ask the Man Who Knows

Mention Bill Veeck's name in Chicago and fans automatically think "White Sox." That's natural, because Barnum Bill, one of the game's truly great showmen, produced two hit shows on the South Side—the Go-Go Sox of 1959, the last pennant-winning team on either side of town, and the 1977 Hit Men, who provided lots of thrills, but no postseason payoff.

But Veeck literally grew up in Wrigley Field. His dad, William Veeck, Sr., was president of the Cubs, so young Bill got to pal around with legendary slugger Hack Wilson, go to spring training on Catalina Island, off the coast of Southern California, with fun-loving manager Jolly Cholly Grimm and his band of free-spirited players, and most of all, soak up his lifelong love of baseball.

It was Veeck, borrowing the idea from a minor-league ballpark in Indianapolis, who planted the ivy on Wrigley Field's outfield walls in 1937.

"We did the job of stringing the wires and hanging bittersweet with ivy on them basically overnight, because the Cubs were coming back from a road trip," Veeck told me. "Bob Dorr [veteran Wrigley groundskeeper] and his crew worked with me until the sun came up to get it done."

Veeck's most-remembered stunt was thumbing his nose at pompous fellow owners in 1951 by sending midget Eddie Gaedel , wearing No. 1/8, up to pinch hit for the St. Louis Browns. When I see the ivy, though, I figure that should stand as his permanent bequest to all baseball fans. No wonder Veeck never lost his interest in the Cubs and his nostalgia for their—and his—ballpark.

"Wrigley Field is a living thing, adapting to its environment," Bill told me once, while we were watching a high school game there. "For the sake of an extra buck, too many owners would willingly destroy traditions like this. My father and I always thought we were custodians for the real owners, the fans. This location was selected for the ballpark because streetcar lines converged here, so people hopped off the trolley and walked to the park."

Wrigleyville, USA

Now, fans come in a steady stream from all over the Midwest, elsewhere around the country and even from overseas. Japan's prime minister threw out a ceremonial first pitch a few years ago, just like a former Eureka College football player and Cubs broadcaster named Dutch Reagan once did. For many of today's visitors, piling off rows and rows of buses, Wrigley Field is more of an attraction than the game itself.

Harry Caray had much to do with that. He created Cubs fans everywhere with his rousing, off-key, seventh-inning rendition of "Take Me Out to the Ball Game," a tradition wisely continued by John McDonough, the marketing director who thinks like a fan. McDonough's Beanie Baby promotions have become a huge lure, adding even non-fans to Wrigley's ticket-window crush.

"We have a situation here unlike anything I know of," McDonough said. "Putting a winning team on the field has to be our first priority, but when it's Wrigley Field, lots of people come just to enjoy the surroundings. They love this place as much as they live and die with the Cubs."

Continuity Counts

The loyalty of Cubs fans has not changed since the 20th century vanished into the mist of time. They still see Wrigley Field as the lone constant among the ever-changing faces on the Cubs' roster, while the front office unveils the latest in an interminable array of rebuilding plans.

Although he spoke these words almost 30 years ago, Chicagoan Dick Karlov sounds like he's saying them in 2003—and probably 3003, if their hallowed playpen is still here then.

"Wrigley Field is about the only thing that hasn't changed since I was a boy," Karlov said. "The ballpark is the main attraction, because it's such a good memory for all of us. There's no nicer place to spend an afternoon in the sun."

Some Players Love It

"Ivy on the walls, crazy fans in the bleachers, not much room outside the foul lines," longtime first baseman Mark Grace said of his affection for Wrigley, despite just two playoffs for the Cubs in his 13 seasons (1989, 1998). "The fans are right on top of you. The pitcher can hear them yelling at him. The Cubs get used to that, just like the crummy weather in April."

One of those Cubs pitchers, Mike Bielecki (1988-91), enjoyed the Wrigleyville ambience so much that he perched during the season in a high-rise apartment near the park. That way, he could check on which way the wind was blowing on days he was due to start.

"Wrigley Field is more fun, because it's not one of those cookie-cutter places," Bielecki said. "The fans are the 10th man for us. Every game is an event, like a Michael Jackson concert."

For perennial Gold Glover Ryne Sandberg, the Wrigley mystique was easy to define. "Tradition," Ryno said. "Year after year, it goes on. Fans react to us and we react to them. In a small park like this, it keeps building."

Lots of Cubs managers also realized the fans' fervor gave them an edge. Leo Durocher had ways of whipping them into a frenzy, but Don Zimmer and Jim Frey were content to watch and admire the pandemonium in the stands.

"Day ball, night ball, it doesn't matter," Zimmer said. "There's no place that can match Wrigley Field. It's just one of the few old shrines that still belong to the fans."

Frey, a real traditionalist, couldn't conceal his disdain for the cookie-cutter plague of round stadiums with artificial turf that sprang up like weeds in both leagues.

"Baseball as we knew it is not played in those parks," Frey said. "On a field with a carpet, it's a different game. Instead of swinging at the ball, batters slap at it, trying to bounce one 30 feet in the air and beat it out. If I had to watch games like that, I wouldn't be a baseball fan."

The Voices of Experience

Jack Brickhouse found out early that Wrigley Field was special, long before he knew most of his working life would be spent there.

"I first came to the park on a train with a couple of hundred people when I was a young man-on-the-street radio interviewer in Peoria," Brickhouse recalled. "My introduction to Wrigley was watching Zeke Bonura [later a White Sox first baseman] beat the Cubs with a home run for the New York Giants. It never occurred to me that I'd be a witness to so many wonderful things in this place.

"Even then, it was so intimate that you felt right at home. I once told [Cubs owner] P. K. Wrigley that I didn't enjoy games nearly as much in other parks. He stopped me in my tracks by saying, 'Jack, other cities have baseball stadiums. We have a real ballpark.'"

Because he stepped into the TV booth when he came over from the White Sox in 1982, Harry Caray became the pied piper for new generations of Cubs fans from every nook and cranny of America.

Brickhouse's radio and TV voice lured them to Chicago ballparks from surrounding states, but both men agreed that Wrigley Field was the end of the rainbow.

"Day baseball and the compact size set Wrigley Field apart," Harry pointed out. "Fans can see the expressions on the players' faces and hear what they're saying."

The last word in the Wrigley accolades that overflowed my notebooks belongs to Ernie Harwell. The legendary Detroit Tigers broadcaster had seen them all, old and new, come and go for almost 60 years, so his vote for Wrigley Field carries more weight.

"When this place is gone, there will never be another to replace it," Harwell said.

Cubs Wind! Cubs Wind! (Fans Freeze!)

The wind always blows around Wrigley Field. Even if cold air is not coming from the skies, there's plenty of hot air on that topic in home and visitors' clubhouses and dugouts. Pitchers insist the Wrigley gale blows in, especially when it's their turn to take the mound. Hitters beg to differ, although I can stand at the batting cage any day when there's a breeze, however slight, out toward the fences and watch them uppercut their pregame swings, sometimes without even realizing it.

Wind-trend statistics kept by the Cubs indicate in recent years that it has blown in, toward the plate, almost twice as much as out, toward those inviting bleachers. Either way, it can turn everything hit in the air into a guessing game for the defense and an out-of-control game on the scoreboard. The famous 23-22 Phillies victory over the Cubs on May 1, 1979, is the modern-era horror show on the dangers of pitching in Wrigley when the wind blows out. They combined for 50 hits, 11 of them homers—three by the Cubs' Dave Kingman and a pair, including the 10th-inning winner, from Cub-killer Mike Schmidt.

"I saw the flags blowing straight out, so I pointed to [Cub infielder] Mick Kelleher's No. 20 and told him 'Get ready—it's a 20-20 day,'" Schmidt said after this dual slaughter.

Every spring, northwest winds off Lake Michigan bring biting chill to the ballpark. It's the same Arctic blast, called "The Hawk," that cuts wintertime Michigan Avenue pedestrians almost in half. Andre "Hawk" Dawson learned to cope with it, as all outfielders must, but he didn't like it.

"It affects you at bat, too," Dawson said. "You can get into a bad habit of trying to jerk the ball. I figure, whether the wind blows out or in, it's important to hit for average, not for homers."

Fans love it when the breeze—or gale—is in their faces, of course, because they know the basket of baseballs batting practice pitchers lug to the mound will end up in their laps. Since the game hasn't started yet, they don't have to throw enemy drives back.

Windy Opinions

Everybody talks about the weather, particularly at Wrigley Field. Unlike elsewhere, fans and players can do something about it. Fans bundle up on chilly afternoons, while players pray for the ball to be hit elsewhere. No matter what, it plays on their minds, like this:

Keith Moreland: "Some days, you couldn't shoot a bullet out of Wrigley Field. Other days, my little daughter could hit a wiffle ball out of here."

Don Baylor (early in 2000, his first season as Cubs manager): "I talked to people about how to deal with this before I came here, but there's not much you can do. The wind blew out for the first few innings today, and then it turned around, making this a pitcher's park. By the end of the day [with fog creeping in], you couldn't even see the buildings across the street."

Billy Williams (veteran Cubs left fielder and coach): "You need two teams to play at Wrigley Field. Your power team has to outslug the other guys when the wind blows out. Other days, you have to do whatever you can for runs and take some chances on the bases. If you play in Chicago, you know it'll be warm one day and cold the next, so it's important to stay loose as you can."

Pitcher Rick Sutcliffe (after a windblown 3-1 loss to the Cards in 1994): "More than any other place, this becomes a pitcher's park when the wind blows in. There are no big innings on days like this. If you don't walk anybody and keep the ball in the park, you'll win."

Cubs center fielder Doug Dascenzo (after battling the wind in 1990): "They're hitting everything to me, to my left, to my right, sinking liners. Playing in that wind is like catching a Frisbee. I might be a better Frisbee player before long."

First baseman Matt Stairs (after opening his brief Cubs career by batting .186 in 20 Wrigley Field games and .315 for 20 road games): "When I get out of Wrigley, I get into a good hitter mode."

Stairs is far from the only player who didn't hit in what's supposed to be a hitter's park. And the moans and groans about Wrigley Field didn't stop there. For instance:

Don Kessinger, dependable Cubs shortstop for a dozen years, still believes Wrigley Field's sun burned out the Cubs in their quest for the 1969 NL pennant: "That heat, day after day, drains your energy," said Kessinger, who had his career day two years later, going six for six in Wrigley Field on June 17, 1971. "By August, the regulars were tired, but [manager Leo] Durocher kept us in the lineup every day. When the Mets made their move, we had nothing left."

Jay Johnstone, Cubs outfielder and clubhouse cut-up: "Wrigley Field is the toughest—windy, sunny, rainy. When there's so much glare, you can't see the ball."

Tommy Helms, Reds infielder: "I've seen pitchers discover they had a sore back or a headache when they came out of the dugout and looked at those Wrigley Field flags."

Pete Rose: "Even if you take care of your body, playing day games makes you more tired."

Bill Buckner, Cubs first baseman: "When the Cubs leave Wrigley Field to go on a trip, it takes three games for the hitters to start seeing pitches again."

Hall of Fame Cubs pitcher Ferguson Jenkins: "[Catcher] Randy Hundley lost so much weight in that sun, he needed suspenders to keep his pants from falling down. The players sweated like pigs, but the fans were in the bleachers with their shirts off, getting a tan. It looked more like Oak Street beach."

Cubs pitcher Burt Hooton: "Playing in Wrigley Field, the Cubs will never win a pennant."

Wrigley Rebuttal

Former Cubs general manager Bob Kennedy and ex-Cubs coach and manager Joe Amalfitano were ballplayers in their younger days. Both of these up-front, honest guys knew that players, like the rest of us, look for excuses when they don't perform well. They didn't mind that, but making Wrigley Field the scapegoat for underachievement offended them.

"The problem for the Cubs in 1969 was not too much sun on the field," Kennedy said. "It was all the agents and hangers-on in the clubhouse, trying to make a buck by signing the players up for commercials, endorsements, personal appearances, radio spots and all kinds of time-consuming things. These guys were just too popular."

Amalfitano, a Durocher disciple, managed the Cubs from 1979-81. He felt the same way Ron Santo did about Wrigley Field, defending it from critics. A longtime Dodgers coach after he left Chicago, Pal Joey savored a pregame stroll around his old park when he came to town.

"I enjoy seeing the place come to life," Amalfitano said. "The players say hello, some of the ushers remember me, and when the gates open, those Cubs fans let me know I'm no longer on the right side. They don't care that I love Wrigley Field as much as they do."

The Show Must Go On

Unless it snows—a lot—or the rain turns the outfield into a swimming pool or the wind-chill reading dips to the teens—so frigid that even Ernie Banks would say "Let's play one today!"—the Cubs try to play ball.

Often, the resemblance to actual baseball, the summer game, is purely coincidental. I've sat through many of those icicle tournaments, still chilly despite closed press box windows, wondering why anybody would (a) play or (b) watch a game under such conditions. And I still miss Jack Brickhouse, who never closed the windows in his booth, flinging open the press box door to yell at the writers, "Open those windows, you hothouse flowers!"

Hard as it was to type or take notes with frozen fingers, I managed to do both while the Cubs battled the elements and the opposition, frequently losing that doubleheader. I was there on a chilly day in June, 1972, when the Pirates completed a three-game sweep that signaled the beginning of the end of that season's Cub playoff hopes. The wind played tricks on them, turning Billy Williams's blast to center into a just-missed homer and transforming Willie Stargell's slice to left into a double.

"The wind just brought it back across the line, from foul to fair," left fielder Williams said of Stargell's bloop hit.

"Then it took one bounce and spun foul again, right in the clubhouse door."

That wasn't a typical Wrigley Field day, mainly because there seems to be no such thing. The wind blows in, out, crossways, sideways or sometimes all of the above, changing with the weather and temperature from inning to inning. I recall a drop of 20 degrees in 10 minutes, with fog swirling over the scoreboard to blot out the bleachers and turn a sunny afternoon into the British moor scenario for a Sherlock Holmes mystery. The wind wasn't the problem on July 4, 1988, when the Cubs built a quick 12-4 lead over the Pirates, only to stagger the rest of the way through a windblown 12-9 victory. The Cubs launched four homers into the wind, then committed four errors, three in a bizarre ninth inning.

"Losing this one would have been hard to handle," said Cubs manager Jim Riggleman, between clenched teeth.

Generations of Cubs fans, players and managers have echoed the same sentiments. Take the snow bowl on April 27, 1973. The Bears had fled Wrigley Field for Soldier Field three years earlier, but this seemed like a replay of them vs. the San Francisco 49ers, right down to the final score—Niners 7, Bears 3.

Wrigley Field was home to the Bears for many years, until their 1971 shift to Soldier Field. They're practicing in 1963, preparing to beat the New York Giants, 14-10, for their final NFL championship under coach George Halas, while workers try to thaw out the frozen turf.

Actually, it was Giants 7, Cubs 3, but at least the shivering fans didn't have to stick around to the bitter—very bitter—end.

"You expect Chicago to be cold in the spring, but not this cold," grumbled the Giants' Willie McCovey.

Some years, the chilblains hang around all spring and into the summer. Such was the case in 1990, frustrating the Cubs' efforts to start fast in defense of the division title they had won a year earlier. Instead, the '90s got off to a dull thud, and the Cubs made the playoffs just once in the decade, although it took a one-game wild card playoff victory over the Giants in 1998 to get them there.

It hurt at the box office, as well. A downpour washed out the May 25, 1990, weekend series opener with Houston, dampening an advance sale of 33,000. Sunshine would have lured a full house to the Friendly Confines, but the drenched Cubs had to huddle in their clubhouse, brooding about the gloomy skies.

"This is the worst spring I can remember in Chicago," said second baseman Ryne Sandberg. "Normally, things get better in May. Not necessarily hot, but at least you get some playable conditions. When the temperature got up to the 80s in April, we were on the road."

Let There Be Lights

With all the problems during Wrigley Field's unpredictable and sometimes unendurable daytimes, you might think that the 1988 installation of lights would have been met with unanimous approval. Think again.

Before it finally happened, in 1988, a Civil War of sorts convulsed Chicago, spreading from the North Side throughout this toddlin' town—even into White Sox territory—thence to the suburbs and downstate Illinois. Before long, a couple of Chicago mayors, the city council, the state legislature and the courts got involved in a modern-day opera, pitting the mammoth Tribune Company, owner of the Cubs, against a small but determined band of urban guerillas, who cleverly dubbed themselves C.U.B.S. The acronym translated into Citizens United for Baseball in Sunshine—get it?

This battle royale raged in every street, every alley, every lamppost, every saloon and every patch of turf in Wrigleyville, the square mile of teeming, turbulent neighborhood surrounding Wrigley Field. It was an all-out struggle, featuring lots of nose-to-nose combat between adamant *Tribune* executives and vehement residents. Naturally, enough legal briefs got filed to provide plentiful yacht payments for flotillas of lawyers.

The whole affair should have become a musical comedy, if not a hilarious sketch by the Second City troupe, with John Belushi portraying Cubs general manager Dallas Green. The death knell for C.U.B.S deserved a score by Verdi— Giuseppi, not Bob. The little guys probably knew from the start that they couldn't prevail against the *Tribune*'s bottomless barrel of clout, but they went down fighting.

Unwittingly, I got the ball rolling on this drama. Soon after William Wrigley, Jr., ended more than 60 years of the gum family's domain by selling the Cubs in 1981 for a mere $21 million, I was assigned to probe the burning question: Would the *Tribune* defy tradition by installing lights in Wrigley Field, the last big-league park without them?

My quest led to Andy McKenna, a Chicago executive with unlimited connections, in and out of the sports world. I soon discovered that the dictionary definition of the word "clout" should have been accompanied by McKenna's picture. We sat down for a lengthy Q-and-A session, and the result was a banner headline atop the front page—the lead story in the news section, not sports—in the next morning's *Chicago Tribune*. It said: NO LIGHTS IN WRIGLEY FIELD: MCKENNA.

Seven years later, the Cubs played their first night game in Wrigley Field. The intrigue, arm-twisting, backroom wheeling and dealing and political power plays that transformed "NO LIGHTS" to "LIGHTS" is indescribable, so I won't try to describe it. Personally, I knew the no-lights game was over when the *Tribune* started playing hardball on its editorial page. All it took on February 10, 1988, was a reference to "political bums" and a blunt threat to move the Cubs out of Chicago. A few months later, the first bank of light towers was being lowered into place on Wrigley's roof.

Same Battlefield, New War

The crusade to control what will happen in and around Wrigley Field goes on unabated. With the park selling out, day and night, the demand for tickets finds almost all of its 39,111 seats filled with fannies almost all the time. Despite their disastrous 67-96 record in 2002, a finish 30 games behind division-winning St. Louis, the Cubs drew an amazing 2,693,096 for only 78 dates, an average of 34, 527.

The Tribune Company's proposed solution to shoehorn more people into the beloved bandbox is to expand the bleachers, adding about 2,000 seats. That would rake in another $3 million at the gate—almost enough to pay the salary of newly acquired catcher Damian Miller, plus a few hundred of the shiny new baseballs Sammy Sosa propels into those bleachers in batting practice and when the game starts.

They also want to play more than the 18 night games per season permitted under the original "let there be lights" agreement. Predictably, neighborhood groups were up in arms about both projects, this time with a powerful ally on their side. Richard M. Daley, who wields his mayoral mallet more subtly, although just as effectively, as his father, Richard J. Daley, Chicago's original "Da Mare," balked at giving carte blanche to the *Tribune.*

The mayor also insisted that community groups get input, somewhere short of veto power, into all Wrigley renovations. The simmering controversy over rooftop seats across the street, enabling apartment owners to charge fancy prices for status seekers to upstage the peasants in the bleachers, escalated when the Cubs installed what they called "windscreens," although everybody knew they were view blockers.

Add the hot potato of pending landmark status for Wrigley Field, making alterations and/or additions much more difficult, if not impossible. It adds up to more quandaries for this venerable showplace than the Cubs have faced on the field for decades. That's a whole lot of problems. Or, as Harry Caray might say, "You Can't Get It Done at the Old Ballpark."

It All Happens Here

Comedian Red Buttons said it best years ago, starting his TV show by chanting "Strange Things Are Happening." Long before Buttons, the Cubs were flipping their lids in Wrigley Field, a place where unfathomable goings-on go on so often that Cubs fans are surprised when something strange does not happen daily, or nightly.

Maybe a lot of trouble would have been avoided if everybody felt like Philip K. Wrigley, the Cubs owner who paid for a full-page newspaper ad to defend his embattled manager, Leo Durocher. Wrigley always had qualms about lights in the park named for his father.

"If a louse like me put in lights, it would wreck the neighborhood," P. K. predicted.

Actually, what night games did for Wrigleyville was to accelerate the boom that began with general manager Dallas Green's "New Tradition" in the 1980s. The Cubs didn't get much better in the standings, except for 1984 and 1989, but the spruced-up ballpark lured more and more cash customers, triggering bonanzas for neighboring bars, restaurants, stores and shops. Housing prices went through the roof, as well, especially for dwellings and apartments with rooftop views of Cubs games.

Despite the boom, what Cubs fans inside or outside Wrigley Field saw ranged from bad baseball to bizarre antics to magic moments. Such tales are legendary, like these:

Cubs rookie Burt Hooton's no-hitter against Philadelphia on April 16, 1972, almost was gone with the wind, but the frigid gale deflated Bull Luzinski's blast, enabling Rick Monday to nab it at the wall.

The fickle Wrigley breeze also saved Ken Holtzman's no-hitter against Atlanta on August 19, 1969. When Braves slugger Hank Aaron unloaded in the seventh inning, Billy Williams sprinted to the fence, expecting to watch The Hammer's sure homer soar high over his head. Instead, the ball curved back into the park, just enough for the Cubs' left fielder's frantic leap to pluck it out of the ivy.

Fortunately, the wind was no deterrent to Gary Gaetti's two-run homer on the night of September 28, 1998, clinching the Cubs' only postseason berth in that decade.

Stan Musial's 3,000th hit on May 13, 1958; Pete Rose's 4,191st hit, on September 10, 1985, tying Ty Cobb's supposedly unmatchable all-time record. Both the Cards and Reds wanted their superheroes to reach those pinnacles at home, but it happened in Wrigley Field.

So did Sammy Sosa's historic 60th and 61st home runs in three separate years (1998-99 and 2001), creating a six-pack of ecstasy for Cubs fans everywhere. Tradition is so much a part of this game that even though Mark McGwire already had surpassed Babe Ruth's 1927 record of 60 homers (and Barry Bonds far eclipsed it with 73 in 2001) there was special significance in Slammin' Sammy's three-peat besting of the Babe.

For Cubs fans everywhere, whether they've lived the pregame excitement at Clark and Addison or merely shared it vicariously on TV, this park is baseball's answer to Disneyland.

CHAPTER 7

"Hey! Hey!" and "Holy Cow!"

I n the beginning, the written word was much more important to baseball than the spoken word. Not any more, though the change was gradual.

For most of the 20th century, the Baseball Writers Association of America ruled press boxes in big-league parks, with veto power over who got in and who didn't. Tape recorder-toting radio people were unwelcome, and shoulder-mounted TV cameras hadn't been invented when I first encountered Elmer, the burly Andy Frain usher who served for years as guardian of the narrow, cramped old Wrigley Field press box, next to the third base catwalk.

Even then, Jack Brickhouse on TV and Vince Lloyd, paired with Lou Boudreau, on radio were closing the gap rapidly. With the explosion of interest in the Cubs during and after that 1969 season in the sun, notwithstanding their September in the tank, the media crush in the clubhouse and on the field mushroomed to Lake Shore Drive traffic-jam proportions. It was merely the opening pitch for what happened when Harry Caray jumped ship from the White Sox, taking over the Cubs' TV booth in 1982.

And that wasn't all the Holy Cow! man took over. Already a cult figure in decrepit Comiskey Park, Harry had the South Side in his hip pocket and was anxious to prove that there was room for the rest of Chicago. In the next 15 years, he did much better than that. Before long, the Cubs were one of America's favorite acts, with him as the ringmaster and the headliner, all rolled into one charismatic package.

But Jack Brickhouse got the ball rolling much earlier, opening an era by describing WGN's first Wrigley Field telecast on April 16, 1948, when the White Sox beat the Cubs 4-1 in a City Series matchup. For five decades, his voice probably was one of the most-recognized ones within reach of WGN's powerful radio and TV signals. In the summertime during the 1950s, '60s, '70s and on into the '80s, it was impossible to walk down any street in Chicago or its booming boondocks without hearing Brickhouse's voice, resonating loud and clear from open windows in house after house: "Back she goes! Back, back . . .Hey! Hey! Attaboy, Ernie! Whee!"

Cornball? Maybe. But it was vintage Chicago, an echo that hangs on in memory vaults inside the heads of just about everybody who grew up around these parts after World War II. Caray's signature routine, warbling "Take Me Out to the Ball Game" in his rasping voice during the seventh-inning stretch, was derided as a vaudeville show by some media sophisticates, as well. But the people who professed to be too hip to enjoy such Wrigley Field window dressing made up a tiny minority.

A pair of Chicago aces, Jack Brickhouse and Ernie Banks, man the WGN microphones. They became lifelong friends as soon as Ernie joined the Cubs in 1953.

The vast and far-from-silent majority loved Harry even more outside his TV booth. They still do, even though he's been gone since Feb. 18, 1998.

We're Still Wild About Harry

In Chicago sports history, there have been lots of superstars. Only two of them in my time became megastars: Michael Jordan and Harry Caray.

An unlikely pairing, the pudgy announcer and the magnificent athlete. About the only thing they had in common was that both of them came from elsewhere to become the two biggest names in Chicago. And not just in sports. Caray and Jordan, Jordan and Caray. The biggest names—period. Yet if it came to a one-on-one showdown between them, I could pick a clear winner.

Harry Carabina. That was his real name, but nobody remembers Cary Grant's real name was Archibald Leach, either. Accept no substitutes. Harry was the one and only.

I first met him in 1971, the night he came to town to take a bow at the annual Chicago baseball writers' dinner. Instead, he took the spotlight and held it until the day he died. Non-native Harry was Chicago, in the same wonderful, inexplicable way that Mayor Richard J. Daley, a Chicagoan by birth, was Chicago.

"There were only two big names in St. Louis—Stan Musial and me," Harry told me that night in '71, after wowing the baseball banquet with the new routines that never got old for the next 28 years. Caray went on and on, telling me more and more and still more than I thought fans might want to know about him. Boy, was I wrong. Harry then embarked on the first of hundreds of what would become his legendary Rush Street bar-hopping tours, greeting cabbies, waitresses, bartenders, fellow night owls and just plain fans with equal-opportunity gusto. His modus operandi never varied: waving, signing autographs, shaking hands and buying a round at every stop. Later, I went on a few of those journeys with Harry, and I never saw him let anyone else pick up a bar tab.

Around dawn on that first night, the time he got to his permanent Chicago home base, the Ambassador East hotel,

Author Bob Logan, left, with Harry Caray.

Harry had picked up the paper with the story I'd written about him hours earlier. He promptly sat down and wrote me a note, now one of my most prized sports souvenirs, ending with the words, "We will have a tall one soon."

Well, Harry and I had lots of tall ones, along with more than a few short ones, over the next couple of decades. Some of the charges leveled by Caray's critics, mainly that he was a shameless self-promoter, might have been true. For me, it came down to the undeniable fact that Harry promoted baseball, first, last and always. He was a tonic for the game, a goodwill ambassador for Chicago and a morale booster for White Sox and Cubs fans, who certainly needed that after watching their teams play. When Caray switched to the Wrigley Field TV booth in 1982, his powerful personality soon made Cubs fans out of people who had never been near Chicago. Because of him, thousands of them made the trek to the Wrigley throne of St. Harry, oftentimes more to sing along with him at the seventh-inning stretch than to see the game.

Hey, Har-eee!

That was the battle cry of Harry's adoring legions. South Side, North Side, it made no difference. He was the fans' guy, wooing them on the air, charming them in person, and above all, luring them to the place where he really believed, "You can't beat fun at the old ballpark!" Without a doubt, Caray saved the White Sox from bankruptcy and/or getting sold out of town—probably both—in his eventful Comiskey Park decade.

That would have been a hard act for anybody to follow, except him. Then Harry topped himself by almost single-handedly transforming the lowly Cubs into one of America's most beloved sports franchises. How did he do it? Here are some clues:

In 1981, the year before Caray became their TV voice, Cubs cablecasts reached one million households. By 1984, that total had rocketed to over 20 million. Some of that boost could be credited to the Cubs' drive to end their depressing streak of 39 years without a postseason berth. Most of it was pure Harry and the way he re-energized Wrigley Field, whipping increasingly bigger crowds into daily—and since 1988, nightly—frenzies.

Not surprisingly, one of Caray's best friends in Chicago was Butch McGuire, a saloon keeper and proprietor of a wildly popular Division Street singles meet market. He summed up Harry's brand of salesmanship by saying, "If this man sold elephants, I'd have them on my shelves. He's the world's greatest salesman."

Harry's fisherman's net, a broadcast booth staple, allegedly was intended to snare foul balls. Actually, it was another aspect of his genius at showmanship. All Caray had to do was wave the net out the window to trigger a "Hey, Hareee!" roar from the stands.

"When I lower the net, I'm amazed at some of the things people put in it," he told me. "Most of them just send blank pieces of paper for autographs, but I've found keys, phone numbers and even dollar bills. I'd never charge any fan to sign my name for them."

Mild About Harry

Caray's outspoken style ruffled feathers, of course. Many ballplayers complained bitterly about the way he pinpointed blame on the spot when things went wrong. Most of them suffered in silence, although White Sox third baseman Bill Melton once confronted his tormentor in a Milwaukee hotel lobby, and punches nearly were thrown. Harry stood his ground, as he always did, eventually earning grudging respect by never hesitating to face the people he had zinged.

Even Melton joined that chorus after getting a game-winning hit against the Sox, who had traded him to California in 1976.

"That was to win a game for the Angels, not me saying 'Take that, Harry,'" Melton confided to me. "He has a lot of power, and we [the players] get mad at him sometimes, but there's no doubt the fans love him."

That was the key, pure and simple, of Harry's enormous popularity. He loved the way the fans loved him, and he loved them back. Those who dared to attack Harry in Chicago soon discovered they had made a multitude of instant enemies. When he switched to the Cubs in 1982, the whole country tuned in on his wavelength. Caray could say things other broadcasters would have been pilloried for, like "How could a guy born in Mexico lose a pop fly in the sun?" He got away with slips of the tongue, bloopers, malaprops, mangled pronunciations and just plain mistakes, especially after suffering a stroke on Feb. 17, 1987.

When Harry Met Ronnie

Harry might have lost a foot off his fastball, as the pitchers say, in his final years with the Cubs. He didn't lose an inch off his grip on the fans. When he came back to work, just three months after the 1987 stroke, his longtime producer, Arne Harris, switched a phone call to the Wrigley Field TV booth.

"Harry, this is Ronald Reagan," said the President of the United States. "A lot of celebrities filled in during your recovery, but there's no substitute for the real thing."

"What a pleasant surprise," responded Caray in one of the few moments he was at a loss for words.

"Last time we were on the air together, you were playing Grover Cleveland Alexander in a movie."

How Old Harry and Cary?

Caray was as nimble as another fan of his, actor Cary Grant, in declining to get pinned down about his real age. A vintage Hollywood story had some brash Eastern magazine writer sending a telegram to the star, demanding: "How old Cary Grant?" He got a quick reply via Western Union: "Old Cary Grant fine. How you?"

Caray's method was the same one used by Dizzy Dean, a colorful Cardinals pitcher in the 1930s. He gave different interviewers a variety of birth dates, ranging from 1914 to 1920. Shaving a few years off is a common practice among ballplayers, and it worked just as well for the ageless broadcaster.

The Day the Music Died

Those of us who were around Caray in the middle '90s could see his strength diminishing. He never lost his zest for the game until his death. A showman to the end, Harry would have been pleased by the statue of him that was dedicated with full fanfare on Opening Day, April 4, 1998. It was the location that doubtless would have pleased him most—outside the bleachers at the corner of Clark and Sheffield.

Right Town, Wrong Side

"I'm glad I'm here to broadcast White Sox games, instead of the Cubs," Caray quipped in 1971, when he came to Chicago. "By the time I get back from Rush Street, it would be too late to get to Wrigley Field for those day games."

Day or night, he helped us have a lot more fun at any old ballpark. Harry's signature "Holy Cow!", originally a defense mechanism for a young broadcaster to avoid slipping back into the profanity he learned on the streets of St. Louis, became the battle cry for new generations of Chicago fans.

Brick's House a Mansion

Jack Brickhouse was the voice of Chicago sports long before Harry Caray showed up to usher in a new style and a new era of micsmanship. Harry was brash, breezy and bold. Jack was soothing, subtle and serene. Trying to draw comparisons between these two giants of the broadcast business would be as futile as preferring balmy breezes over summer sunshine.

Caray was a man mostly for one season—baseball—although he did other sports, as well. When the game was dull, he suffered along with his listeners. And when things got exciting, he could bring the fans bolt upright in their chairs at home—"Here it is! Heee had a cut! It's in there, a curve, a beauty! There's danger here, Cherie..." And on and on, into the night. Harry's charisma came right through your radio and/or TV set .

Jack Brickhouse? A different story entirely. Even if I could, I wouldn't try to draw parallels between him and Caray. Both were friends, fellow travelers in the sports world, even though they traveled in much loftier circles than I did. Everybody wanted a piece of their fame—and them— because sports, despite all the ways it gets weighted down with the drug, sex and violence baggage that now afflicts our society, still makes grownups feel like kids again. Harry was aware of the power he wielded, and he used it.

So did Jack. But their styles were different, which explains the totally diverse way they called a ballgame. Brickhouse's Cubs reflected his personality—easy-going, ever-hopeful. He was the right man to start announcing Cubs games on WBKB-TV in 1947 for the princely sum of $35 a game. Listeners quickly got the impression he'd gladly do it for free.

Brickhouse was still the right man in 1981, 34 years and more than 5,000 games later, when he described the Cubs' daily doings for the last time on WGN-TV. And he still talked, felt and sounded like someone who would gladly have done all of them for free.

"Bob, the only thing I would change is getting to call the seventh game of a Cubs-White Sox World Series in Wrigley Field," Jack told me when we sat down to tape some of his stories for one of my earlier books. "From a young guy doing 'man on the street' radio interviews in Peoria to sitting down for chats with presidents, kings and even the pope, my career keeps convincing me I'm the luckiest stiff in the world."

He might have sounded like a politician, but he wasn't. The difference between Brickhouse and many politicians was that he was not trying to get elected to anything. His enthusiasm was genuine, just like he was. That's one major reason why a couple of generations in Chicago grew up liking baseball in general and the Cubs in particular. Day baseball had a lot to do with it, too, along with the elevated trains and buses that stopped at Wrigley Field's front door. The fan-friendly ballpark was another drawing card for young people, hooking kids into lifelong espousal of Jack's wait-till-next-year optimism.

So most Cubs fans now in their 50s or even older came to associate baseball with Brickhouse's voice, drifting out of windows on a summer day, from car radios or portables on the beach. He was their Pied Piper—not Pat Pieper—assuring them that the Cubs would get better someday, and that things would get better for them immediately if they came to Wrigley Field.

Ernie Banks on Brick

No wonder there was such a bond between Ernie Banks and Jack Brickhouse. They were two of a kind, peas in a pod. On my all-time, all-cheerful list, they've always been a Top 10 entry. Brickhouse took the 22-year-old rookie under his wing in 1953, as soon as the Cubs bought the kid shortstop from the Kansas City Monarchs. Their friendship was still going strong, right up to August 6, 1998, the day Brickhouse died. Ernie still has a fund of stories about his pal Jack.

"We always knew how lucky we were to be doing what we wanted more than anything else," Banks told me while we were talking about what he wanted to say in his foreword for my book, *So You Think You're a Die-hard Cub Fan.* "Next to Mr. Wrigley [Philip K., the Cubs' owner, who took a chance on signing the slender youngster and always called that move his smartest decision in baseball], Jack was my biggest supporter in Chicago. I always tried to help him out whenever I could, because he did so much for me.

"When I hit a homer in the first inning of the 1960 All-Star Game, it was for him. He was broadcasting the first few innings, so I wanted to give him something to talk about."

That's Gratitude

B rickhouse never came up short in the words department. One of the few times he regretted that was when P. K. Wrigley asked him in 1966 if the Cubs should gamble on hiring Leo Durocher, a man with a rough-and-ready past and a shady reputation.

"I told P. K. to take a chance on Leo," Brickhouse said. "After I while, I could see it wasn't going to work out."

Brickhouse admitted to me privately what he seldom said publicly: Durocher tripped over his own massive ego, eventually getting more caught up in Chicago's social whirl than the fortunes of the struggling Cubs. When the tired club faltered in 1969, on the doorstep of a division title, Leo's bubble burst, even though he hung around for a few more fruitless years.

Man for All Games

Workaholic Brickhouse always needed a mic to talk into, a game to describe and an audience to listen to him. I first met him in 1966, when my 16-year merry-go-round on the Bulls' beat began the day they got an NBA franchise. Naturally, Jack jumped in feet first to help a team few others figured would last long in Chicago. He negotiated a WGN-TV contract with Dick Klein, the colorful pitchman who concocted the Bulls out of thin air, and went on the road with them to do play-by-play. When the Bulls won their first game, pulling an upset in St. Louis, Jack was there to give the newcomers his traditional "Hey! Hey!" salute.

Then there was the trip to Cincinnati (temporary home of the Royals, formerly based in Rochester, N.Y., later the Kansas City-Omaha Kings and now the Sacramento Kings) to do a Bulls game. In the hotel that afternoon, Bulls coach Johnny Kerr maneuvered Brickhouse and me around strategically placed floor lamps to show us his version of that basketball standby, the pick-and-roll play. He did all that and lots more while working a full schedule of Cubs and/or White Sox telecasts and teaming with Chicago columnist Irv Kupcinet for 24 years (1953-76) on Bears play-by-play.

Brickhouse switched gears and seasons with the same unflappable, affable ease. John McDonough, marketing director of the Cubs, has no doubt about his place in broadcasting history.

"Jack was the best ever in Chicago," McDonough asserted. "Not just sports, but in everything, from on-the-spot breaking news to major events like political conventions, interviews with world figures and just plain people. With all of that, he found time to make more charity and fundraising appearances for worthy causes than anybody else. He took everything in stride and he laid the foundation for the Cubs' popularity. Harry Caray spread it all over the country, building on what Brickhouse did."

Jack of All Nations

The first words heard live on an intercontinental telecast were spoken by Brickhouse: "No score in this ballgame." It happened on July 23, 1962, when the Telstar satellite beamed a 90-second glimpse of Wrigley Field, during a Cubs-Phillies game, to Rome, Vienna and Stockholm.

The True Test

Many temperamental celebrities show a phony facade to the public. The people propping them up behind the scenes bear the brunt of preserving the image. That never was the case with Brickhouse.

His crews and cameramen conspired to make Jack's "Hey! Hey!" home run call a household word by flashing the words on the screen while the Cubs hitter circled the bases. And his two closest associates for decades, TV director Arne Harris and WGN sports editor Jack Rosenberg, were unabashed Brickhouse boosters.

"Jack always looked for something in the stands to brighten up the game when things weren't going well on the field," Harris said "He knew when the Cubs were bad, just like the fans did, but he found something good to talk about."

Rosenberg underscored that was the real reason why Brickhouse lasted so long and wore so well with his vast audience.

"Jack Brickhouse was the man you wanted as a friend, a brother, a father or a co-worker," he said.

Lou Can Do

Lou Boudreau did not look like a great athlete, even in his playing days. He had bad ankles, tightly wrapped before every game to ease the constant pain. The shortstop and player-manger did not look like a great competitor, either. In his case, those looks were extremely deceiving.

Long after his career was over, Boudreau's inner fire still burned brightly in the WGN radio booth. He refused to give up on the Cubs, no matter how inept the team or how hopeless that day's deficit. His usual even tones went up a couple of octaves while he told broadcast partner Vince Lloyd what the Cubs should have done in any situation, often the exact reverse of what they actually did. He never lost that zest for the game or that burning desire to win.

Not that he asked other players to do things he couldn't do. In the clutch, with a game or a pennant on the line, few athletes in any sport could come through like Lou Boudreau did.

His WGN tenure was interrupted in 1960, when he switched places briefly with Cubs manager Charlie Grimm. Ed Alsene, my sports editor in Springfield, Illinois, summed up that strange move with a brilliant headline: "GRIMM GETS AIR (WGN); BOUDREAU TO MANAGE CUBS." But there were few Boudreaus left for Lou to manage, because he was one of a kind. When he went back to the radio booth for good in 1961, it was a break for him and a boon for thousands of fans, who listened and learned the right way to play this game.

Lou was pleased when I told him the best entertainment on a Cubs broadcast in those days happened when there was a rain delay. Boudreau would talk baseball with Vince Lloyd and Jack Brickhouse, who were smart enough to toss a question at him, so that he could swat it out of the park. Tapes of those interludes should have been preserved for generations of young players to learn how to hit the cutoff man; how to detect pitchers tipping off pitches by failing to conceal their grip with the glove and a multitude of other subtle skills that keep vanishing in this swing-from-the-heels era.

When Lloyd came to Chicago for the debut of Brickhouse's Broadcast Museum exhibit in 2001, we sat down and talked about those days. Vinny and Lou, a matched set of soft-spoken gentlemen, called each other "Good Kid," a totally accurate sobriquet for them.

"I was constantly amazed by Lou's encyclopedic knowledge of baseball," Lloyd told me. "He taught me a lot. We used to go to the race track on off days. Maybe he couldn't pick the horses too well, but he sure had a handle on what might happen in every situation or any pitch."

Pat Hughes (left) and Ron Santo provide a one-two punch on Cubs radio broadcasts. Hughes's easy-going style blends well with the former Cubs third baseman's emotional approach.

A Home Ron Hitter

Just like he was for the Cubs, Ron Santo is a heavy hitter in the WGN radio booth. His banter with play-by-play announcer Pat Hughes probably kept some frustrated Cubs fans from taking a leap off the Michigan Avenue Bridge into the Chicago River during Don Baylor's depressing two and a half-year managerial tenure. Even eternal optimist Santo might have been tempted to join them at times.

"Yes, it's hard to talk about the Cubs coming up short on the radio, just like it was when I played for them," Santo told me while he was recovering from surgery to remove his right leg, below the knee. "But I learned a lesson in 1969, and it still sticks with me."

Santo was at third base that wonderful, woeful summer, when the Cubs got to third base in their seeming cakewalk to the World Series, only to get hung up there while the New York Mets roared past.

It was a bitter blow to Santo, an emotional Italian, although he knew the Cubs did not blow it, contrary to what many Cubs fans felt then, and still do, more than three decades later. The Mets were simply unbeatable down the stretch, a runaway train that crushed Chicago's hopes like tinfoil on the tracks.

"I was very unhappy until Glenn Beckert [second baseman on that team] convinced me that some things can't be changed, no matter how hard you try. Beck was right. It was just the Mets' year."

That philosophy came in handy when a small sore on his right foot suddenly triggered a life-and-death crisis in June 2002. A lifelong diabetic, Santo had been battling the disease and leading a fight against it, especially to help kids, even before 1974, when his baseball career ended. His courage in that effort surpassed anything he did on the field, where the fiery third baseman never backed away from any opponent.

After electing to lose his left leg, also below the knee, in 2002, Santo felt he would finally earn that long-delayed Hall of Fame welcome. "Devastated" by another rejection, he went to spring training with the same unbeatable optimism.

That's why I've been a Santo fan for a long time, even though writers are not supposed to root. Still, we're human, despite what some ballplayers, many readers and even a few editors might think, and we all have our favorites. My yearly Hall of Fame vote went to Santo as long as he was on the ballot, and I do not believe it was a homer decision on my part. Anyone looking objectively at Santo's stats—344 homers, 1,331 RBI and a .954 fielding average—has to conclude that he compares favorably with George Kell, Pie Traynor and even the great Brooks Robinson, all of them in the Hall.

I'll let fans and old-timers stage that debate. The way Santo came back from every ordeal, even his heart stopping during one of numerous operations, convinces me he belongs. When he came back to resume the good-natured razzing of his friend, Pat Hughes, and walk daily to the Wrigley Field stands to sign pregame autographs, a Chicago winner was back in action.

Santo Stoned

S teve Stone, a practical joker with a keen baseball mind, pulled one on Ron Santo that worked too well.

He arranged a fake press release, declaring that Stone, Harry Caray's former TV sidekick, would move into the WGN radio booth to share analyst duties. When he saw that Santo briefly got taken in by the gag, Stone was remorseful.

"I thought Ronnie and Pat Hughes would get a chuckle out of it," Stone said. "Anybody who knows what Santo has gone through as a diabetic has nothing but respect for him."

Stone's gentle kidding and easy repartee with Harry Caray was a real touch of class, especially after the Chicago icon suffered a stroke in 1987 and came back to work, despite losing a little more of his cutting-edge sharpness with each succeeding year. He had a valuable ally in Wrigley Field's TV booth, because Stone was always ready to pick up the ball with a low-key correction or a timely pun.

"Harry was always No. 1," Steve said. "My job was to back him up, any I could."

He could—and did.

CHAPTER 8

All Are Cubs—
Some Are Flubs

You can't tell the players without a scorecard." That's been the battle cry of countless program peddlers in and around thousands of ballparks for 150 years, give or take a strike-shortened season or two.

Such a sales pitch seldom is necessary for Cubs fans. They know their players, all right. And they take a proprietary interest in any body draped in Cubbie blue, from superstars of the Kerry Wood-Sammy Sosa stripe to such cup-of-coffee trivia questions as Joe Strain (batted .189 in 1981) or Bryan Hickerson (6.82 ERA in 1995). Partly, that's the legacy of Ernie Banks, the most beloved Cub of them all, and still "Mr. Cub" more than 30 years after his 512th—and last—homer for them.

Partly, it's the lure of Wrigley Field, the place where kids get hooked for life on the Cubs, while their parents relive their own youth. Before, during and after games, fans are so close to the field that they can see the players' faces and even hear what they're saying. When the outcome of games no longer is in doubt, my habit for years has been to leave the press box and sit where I can watch the fans' reactions, as well as the final outs.

No need to look at the scoreboard to tell who's ahead. A glance at the faces around me does the trick. Cubs fans have learned to tolerate losing, but unlike their counterparts in New York, Boston or Philadelphia, they seldom vent their frustration on the players. No wonder most Cubs, from cult figures like Sosa, Andre "Hawk" Dawson and Gary "Sarge" Matthews Sr. to raw rookies, get psychic income from performing for such faithful fanatics.

Unfortunately, even that unflagging loyalty has not translated into enough Cubs victories, Cubs playoff berths and the ultimate fan fantasy—a Cubs return to the World Series. Despite the paucity of postseason glory, Cubs fans greeted the dawn of the Dusty Baker era with a renewed burst of optimism. They see new faces on the roster, and a proven winner in new manager Baker, to weld their team into a contender.

In my years on the Cubs scene, I've seen such rosy expectations run smack into a reality roundhouse and get counted out in the '70s, '80s (with two exceptions), '90s (one breakthrough) and the same script so far in the 21st century. Everybody would be happy to see Sosa cap his magnificent career with a game-winning World Series homer, including me.

If it doesn't happen, Cubs fans and I will share good memories of sunny days and fogless nights in the Friendly Confines. Plenty of rain, wind and chill, too. For me, watching hundreds of guys in Cub suits, from Hall of Famers to barely famous, has been more fun than work. With some

Catcher Jody Davis, a Cubs fan favorite, shakes off the punishment that comes with his demanding position. Umpire Bruce Froemming, whose borderline call deprived Milt Pappas of a 1972 perfect game, lends a hand, while trainer John Fierro (right) comes in to assist.

notable exceptions (see chapter 2), they were easy to talk to, deal with and write about. I tried using tape recorders to gather quotes on occasion, but that method didn't work well for me, especially on deadline. Wading through the 90 percent of meaningless postgame cliches ("That was a big win for us," or "I know my teammates are busting their butts for me") to get to one punchy quote is too time-consuming.

Writing 900 to 1,000 words under relentless time pressure, struggling to make it an entertaining, relevant, complete and above all accurate portrayal of the game you're covering, is no easy task. I learned long ago that scribbling gibberish-free words, sentences and sometimes even paragraphs of good quotes in a notebook enabled me to fit them into the story's framework much more efficiently.

Those scribblings are my reward for many years of sportswriting, including this book. One thing I'm proud of is that I have seldom been accused of misquoting a player or manager or taking what they meant to say out of context. Another reason why I enjoy doing this is my belief that these slices of sports history should be preserved and passed along to new generations of readers and fans. Out of all those notebooks, for all those years, here's a glimpse at some of the players I can't forget.

Written in Stone

S teve Stone is one of the most interesting, certainly among the brightest, people I've met in sports. That covers a lot of territory. Ever since the 26-year-old right-hander came to the White Sox in 1973, moving to the Cubs a year later, he brought along an impressive blend of poise and savvy. Unlike most young players, Steve really understood baseball, and he knew how to interpret the game's nuances. So I'm pleased that he came back to WGN-TV's booth in 2003, teaming with Harry Caray's grandson Chip.

It was clear from the outset that this man was going places. While winning the American League Cy Young Award with a 25-7 dream season for Baltimore in 1980, Stone was already a successful restaurateur, with a piece of Chicago's legendary Pump Room and successful operations in Arizona. WGN was smart enough to summon him back to the Cubs in 1983 as the TV interpreter for Harry Caray's entertaining jumble of malaprops, mispronouncements, name mangling and occasional glaring errors.

Stone fielded them all with a smooth blend of humor and insight, playing enough defense in the TV booth to deserve a Gold Glove. I've always wondered why some team (the Cubs, for instance) didn't snap him up as general manager. Maybe it's because his tough-minded analysis of every team's strengths and weaknesses did not paint the unrealistic picture many egotistical owners prefer to hear. Anyway, Stoney's quotes were way ahead of his contemporaries as a player, and they got better as the years went by. A couple of my personal favorites, set in Stone:

"The writers, in their infinite wisdom, were crying for me to be buried in the bullpen," Steve told me in 1979, when his rediscovered forkball turned him almost overnight into one of baseball's best pitchers.

"I've had my differences with Earl Weaver [the Orioles' feisty manager], but he keeps telling me, 'Here's the ball. You're a starting pitcher.' Something had to be done, because I gave up about 15 homers on hanging curveballs. So I thought back to the forkball Fred Martin [former Cubs pitching coach] taught me in 1974."

The results were magical. Struggling with a 6-7 record at the '79 All-Star break, Stone racked up a 30-7 mark over the next one and a half seasons, baffling hitters with his new out pitch. He stopped losing games, although he kept the quick wit that set him apart from the herd.

"I don't hang around the clubhouse much after games," he said. "Being surrounded by a bunch of hairy-legged guys in their underwear never was my idea of fun."

Dream Sequence

When Don Zimmer was their manager (1988-91), the punchless Cubs scored even less than Rodney Dangerfield. Zim had to try about everything except stealing first base to generate some offense, so imagine his elation on June 8, 1990, when the Cubs poured across 11 runs in the third inning to pulverize the Phillies, 15-2. His reaction?

"I slapped myself to make sure I was awake," Zimmer said.

An even bigger surprise during that rout was shortstop Shawon Dunston's long-awaited 100th career base on balls. Dunston usually started swinging in the on-deck circle and didn't stop, even if the pitch was in the dirt or over his head. He went into the game with only 98 walks in 2,420 at-bats—an astronomical ratio of one for every 25.2 trips—but strolled twice to reach the century mark.

"I took a lot of razzing," the grinning Dunston confessed. "After the second walk, they tried to give me the ball."

Perfectly True

If anybody knows anything about all-around pitching, it's 43-year-old Mike Morgan, who's been all around both circuits, into his fourth big-league decade. There's no truth to the rumor the ex-Cub was the starting pitcher in the 1839 game of town ball in Cooperstown, New York, when Abner Doubleday allegedly invented baseball, but he's performed for almost everybody else, from coast to coast. The durable right-hander kept on going into the 21st century with the attitude that served him well during his two stints with the Cubs (1992-95 and 1998).

"I got a pitch up and he hurt me," Morgan said after yielding a homer to the Phillies' Dave Hollins in Wrigley Field. "We're not perfect. If pitchers were perfect, there wouldn't be any hitters."

Raffy Trade Daffy?

Cubs fans can't help wondering what might have happened in the '90s—and beyond—if the Cubs hadn't made a bad trade on December 5, 1988. They shipped first baseman-outfielder Rafael Palmiero, along with pitchers Jamie Moyer and sore-armed lefty Drew Hall, to the Texas Rangers. Tough-luck Hall opened some eyes in his Cubs debut when he fanned 10 White Sox batters in seven innings on May 19, 1986, but never lived up to his promise.

Palmiero and Moyer sure did—unfortunately, elsewhere. In between making semi-raffish Viagra commercials, Raffy became one of baseball's most consistent power hitters. Both he and Sammy Sosa entered 2003 looking to join the prestigious 500-homer club and tie the major-league record of nine straight seasons with 35 or more home runs, held by Jimmie Foxx. The Cubs got reliever Mitch Williams and some guys named Joe in that Texas horse trade, gaining a 1989 division title on the Wild Thing's 36-save heroics, but giving up who knows how many shots at the impossible dream—a World Series in Wrigley Field.

Just suppose, drooling Cubs fans, that your team had kept Palmiero and Moyer and stopped nursing nickels long enough to re-sign Greg Maddux in 1992. That was the same year they stole a young outfielder named Sammy Sosa from the White Sox. Dream on.

But way back in '87, when Palmiero was just trying to stick on the Cub roster, starting that season in the minors was a jolt to the future Hall of Famer.

"I was not used to failing," said the youngster, who was a college teammate of slugger Will Clark and future White Sox closer Bobby Thigpen at Mississippi State. "I learned I have to earn my job up here."

While Palmiero and Moyer were doing just that in the American League, Maddux had to build an extra mantelpiece for his Atlanta collection of Cy Young trophies. The Cubs, even with Sosa's budding superstardom, got sentenced to another might-have-been decade. Singles (and doubles) hitter Mark Grace was a fancy-fielding first baseman, but the Cubs got to first base in the pennant race just once with him, backing into a 1998 wild card spot, only to back out of the playoffs even faster.

Meanwhile, Palmiero was wearing out AL basepaths with his home run trot, Moyer's dipsy-do soft stuff kept baffling hitters, and Maddux joined Tom Glavine and John Smoltz to pitch a dynasty teepee for the Braves.

Cubs Get Tapped Out

Pitchers seldom finish what they start nowadays. Still, Cubs fans couldn't blame Kevin Tapani for wanting to change Leo Durocher's famous quote to "Nice guys finish best." One of the best people I encountered on the Cubs beat, the veteran right-hander deserved lots more help than he got from the bullpen in his five North Side years.

Tapani kept the Cubs in the game for most of his 128 starts. Relievers frequently provided little or no relief, especially in 2000, when he started 30 games, left with the lead six times and the score tied four times, only to get a no-decision in all 10 of those. Pitchers with 20-victory seasons usually can look back on a couple of starts when they trailed, got the hook and still ended up as the winner because their team rallied. Not Tapani.

So, especially for a man with ample reason for clubhouse tantrums, the former White Sox hurler showed remarkable restraint by not hurling gloves, bats, the postgame food spread, or even epithets at a handy target—the media converging around his locker. No matter how tough the loss, Tapani never ducked us, dealing with all questions and inquisitors in the same even-tempered tone.

"Getting mad at you guys won't make me feel better," Tap told me in the middle of his personal 12-game losing streak that stretched for 15 starts, from June 24, 1999, until April 28 of the following season.

"Besides, it can't change what happened. Everybody in this clubhouse shared the credit when we made the playoffs [in 1998]. You can't put the blame for losing on one guy, either."

Nobody blamed Tapani when the Cubs sneaked into that one-game wild card playoff with the Giants in '98. He stepped up to become the ace of the staff after Kerry Wood missed the final month with the elbow misery and eventual surgery that kept him out of action until May 2, 2000. Tapani (19-9), Steve Trachsel (15-8) and Wood (13-6) combined for 47 victories—more than half of the Cubs' total of 90.

Sadly, they got no more in an 0-3 first-round playoff wipeout by the Braves and old pal Greg Maddux.

Far above and beyond his 48-48 record with the Cubs, Tapani's ability to put things in perspective made him a quiet clubhouse leader and a teacher for Wood and other young pitchers. He was at his best after one of the worst losses of them all. That was in Cincinnati on May 7, 1999, when Tapani worked a gritty eight innings, turning a 2-1 lead over to Cubs closer Rod "Shooter" Beck. The Shooter shot only the Cubs, blowing the save and the game to the Reds on Barry Larkin's two-out, two-run double. Tapani's response should have been taped to become mandatory listening for every rookie pitcher.

"I was driving on an empty tank in the eighth inning, so I can't second-guess Jim [Cubs manager Riggleman]," he said. "We did everything by the book, the way a winning team should all the time. The starter [himself] got the ball to Rod with the lead in the ninth. That's how we made it to the postseason last year, and I don't see why it can't work again."

A major reason why it didn't was the string of injuries plaguing Tapani near the end of his career. He was far from through when the White Sox mistakenly gave up on him, despite a 13-10 record in 1996, but the new Cub's debut was delayed by finger surgery in 1997. Afterwards, shoulder, back and knee problems put Tap on the disabled list at various times, curtailing his Cub starts. None of those ailments hurt worse than Game 2 of the 1998 NL playoff in Atlanta, where had a 1-0 lead until Javier Lopez homered to tie it in the ninth inning and the Braves won, 2-1, in the 10th.

Kerry Wood's right arm—perhaps the deadliest weapon in Chicago sports since Bobby Hull's slap shot. Photo courtesy of the Chicago Cubs.

"No regrets about that game or anything that happened in Chicago," Tapani said after the Cubs declined to pick up his $4 million salary option for 2002. "I'll never forget how the guys stuck with me through the [12-game] losing streak. They were beginning to press, because everybody was aware of the streak and nobody wanted to make a mistake when I pitched."

Zonk Sniffs at Cubs

Keith "Zonk" Moreland could be counted on for two things when he played for the Cubs from 1982-87. The former Texas defensive back, nicknamed for Zonker Harris of "Doonesbury" fame, never stopped hustling—or telling the truth. That's why he was a fan favorite in 1984, while the Cubs had them dancing in the streets by coming within one game of a 1945 World Series rematch with the Detroit Tigers.

Moreland refused to alibi during a nightmarish 0-3 playoff weekend in San Diego that turned the dream into a nightmare. He was still telling it like it was two years later, with the self-destructing Cubs already 20 1/2 games behind the Mets, before the end of June.

"Right now, we stink," Moreland confessed, lamenting a 7-4 loss on June 29, 1986, to the Mets and Cub-killer Dwight Gooden. "I can't say one person's not getting the job done. It's all of us, including me, I'm right down there with the rest of the team.

"Fortunately, every season has a second half. If we want to stay in Chicago, we better make the most of it."

Moreland's premonition proved accurate. The staggering Cubs, already out of the race, were laboring under their third manager before the season's midpoint. Jim Frey, the toast of the town only two years earlier—at least until that traumatic playoff collapse in San Diego—stepped down early in 1986, with coach John Vukovich taking the reins for two games. For the record, Vukovich split his pair of decisions, joining an exclusive Cubs managerial club.

He became just one of three pilots in the franchise's first 128 years to finish with an even .500 record, joining Jim Lefebvre (162-162 in 1992-93) and Bob Ferguson (30-30 in 1878). A few notable exceptions who barely made it to the plus side were Leo Durocher (535-526 in 1966-72) and Don Zimmer (265-258 in 1988-91).

General manager Dallas Green, a self-styled baseball genius, made sure the Cubs wouldn't repeat their 1984 heroics, replacing the Frey-Vukovich regime by thumbing through a big-league executives' directory to come up with Gene Michael, a Yankees lifer. Michael knew little about the National League and less about Chicago, so he was doomed from the start, fleeing town before the next losing season ended.

Sutter Splits Foes' Bats

B ruce Sutter's split-fingered out pitch got the Cubs out of numerous jams in his 1976-80 reign as bullpen king. He racked up 133 saves, with a season-high 37 in 1979. Yet Cubs fans got on him when he didn't close the deal every time out. The jeers were loudest in '78, with

Sutter suffering through a slump while the Cubs fizzled at the end, an all-too-familiar scenario.

"Hey, Herman—go kick Sutter in the ass!" a frustrated Wrigley Field spectator bellowed at rotund Cubs manager Herman Franks, himself nearing the end of his final season at the helm.

The same sort of unrest broke out in the Cubs' clubhouse, as well. Ken Holtzman, author of two no-hitters for them in 1969 and again in 1971, was finding it hard to keep his cool in the lefty's second term on the pitching staff.

"We haven't had a clubhouse fight since Ron Santo tried to choke that despicable Leo Durocher," Holtzman recalled of that memorable blowup on August 23, 1971, with Durocher barking, "I didn't realize you guys hated me so much," then ripping off his uniform before general manager John Holland had to talk him out of quitting on the spot.

"Leo wanted respect, so he asked the players to speak up, and Santo, Milt Pappas and other guys told him what they really thought about him," said the quiet man, Billy Williams.

Holtzman, no fan of Durocher, held his tongue in that uprising, but blew up when he heard Cubs players talking of sharing third-place money with Montreal at the tail end of 1979.

"I almost went crazy," Holtzman said. "With a month left, some of these guys were quitting."

Sutter refused to give up on himself or the team. He added 32 victories to those 133 saves, but the Cubs refused to yield when an arbitrator decided their closer was worth $900,000, so they dealt him to St. Louis after the 1980 season for Leon Durham, Ken Reitz and Ty Waller. Shrugging off shoulder problems, Sutter helped the Cards win the 1982 World Series, then signed a whopping $25 million contract with Atlanta, only to get his career string of saves cut short at 300 by that stubborn injury.

Ironically, Sutter is best remembered in Chicago for getting victimized by ex-teammate Ryne Sandberg on June 23, 1984. Ryno tied the game with a ninth-inning solo homer off Sutter, then did it again with a two-run shot in the 10th. Amid the hysteria that turned Wrigley Field into a lunatic asylum when the Cubs won, 12-11, few noticed that the Cubs reliever who gave up two runs to the Cards in the top of the 10th was Lee Smith, the new bullpen savior. Baseball is, indeed, a funny game, but Sutter kept his cool-headed approach, despite the constant pressure that knots most relief pitchers' stomachs.

"I'll never change," he told me during his first season in St. Louis. "I have a businesslike approach, because this is a business."

And much more often than not, Sutter's diving-bombing splitter gave hitters the business.

North vs. South

Ron Coomer, a born and bred Chicago fan, spent most of his career in the American League. But for the 2001 season, he was part of a turnabout that had Cubs fans dreaming of a Wrigley Field October. From a dismal 65-victory showing in Don Baylor's managerial debut, they spurted to 88-74, finishing just five games behind division-winning Houston.

Pennant fever was a raging epidemic on June 8, with the cocky Cubs, 15 games over .500 at 36-21, fresh from a wild weekend Wrigley Field sweep of the Cards that put them in first place—First Place!—by five full games, heading to Comiskey Park for a showdown with the White Sox. If only moments like that could be bottled to get Cubs fans through all those dreary might-have-been winters, Wrigleyville's quality of life would quadruple over its normal state of perpetual optimism, even in the worst of times. And nobody was savoring that brief shining moment more than Coomer, although he confessed to being a boyhood Sox fan.

"This is really big," Coomer said, perched in the visitors' Comiskey Park dugout while the stands filled with a 50-50 blend of Cubs and Sox fans, proving that oil and water sometimes can mix. "All weekend, while we were winning three straight from the Cardinals, you could feel the electricity building up in Wrigley Field. Our fans were happy about the sweep, but we could see those 'Bring on the Sox' signs they were holding up.

"When I was a kid here, Cubs vs. Sox was the only game in town, even if it was just an exhibition. The bragging rights meant a lot more to the fans than they did for the players. Now that these games count in the standings, it just adds more excitement. This is really fun. The whole city is plugged in, taking sides and arguing baseball."

Mac's Comeback

Lloyd McClendon showed some promise and some punch for the 1989 Cubs, batting .286 with a dozen homers and 40 RBIs. A year later, hitting a lowly .177, the career benchwarmer got shipped to Pittsburgh for a lefty pitcher named Michael Pomeranz, who never made it to the Cubs. A Gary, Indiana native, McClendon caught the eye of big-league scouts by homering in five at-bats and walking in the other five at the 1971 Little League World Series.

But he had to struggle through almost nine years in the minors before the Reds finally called him up. The way the charismatic McClendon handled that adversity stamped him as a man with leadership potential. Besides, he had seen almost all the right and wrong ways to handle every strategic situation down there in the bushes, filing away that information for future use.

"Life is funny," McClendon reflected when the Cubs gave up on him in 1990. "It hasn't been a good year for me, but I want to go help the Pirates win some games. "

Now, the ex-Cub is doing that as Pittsburgh's manager. He spoiled Opening Day 2002 in Wrigley Field by steering the Pirates to a 2-1 victory, continuing the downward spiral that cost manager Don Baylor his job on July 5, just before the All-Star break. Bruce Kimm, well-liked skipper of the Iowa farm club, got summoned to shuffle the lineup the rest of the way, but couldn't stop the bleeding for the 67-95 Cubs.

An Eerie Omen

Little was made of it at the time, but a year later, some fans recalled what had happened to Cardinals pitcher Darryl Kile in Wrigley Field on July 27, 2001. A line drive by Robert Machado of the Cubs glanced off Kile's glove and hit him in the face. Somehow, the veteran scrambled after the ball and threw Machado out at first base, preventing a run from scoring. He collapsed on the infield grass, but insisted on coming out for the sixth inning before going to the hospital for stitches.

So manager Tony La Russa and the rest of the Cards knew something was wrong when Kile, a team leader and an intense competitor, did not show up at Wrigley Field on June 22, 2002, the day before he was scheduled to start against the Cubs. Only 33, Kile was found dead in his hotel room, the victim of congenital heart disease. That game got canceled, but the Cubs won, 8-3, the next day, although the shock of Kile's death cast a pall over fans and players alike. For once, the ferocious Cubs-Cards rivalry took a back seat to shared sadness.

"The way the Cubs fans reacted, telling our players how sorry they were about Darryl, showed me a lot of class," La Russa said.

Center of Attention

Could Corey Patterson be the center fielder the Cubs have been seeking...and searching...and scrambling for, almost all the way back to the days of Handy Andy Pafko, their outstanding middle gardener in the 1945 World Series? They've known all along, ever since making Patterson their top 1998 draft choice, that the fleet youngster has all the tools, including flashes of tremendous power.

But Wrigley's center field patch of turf has been torn up for so many years by hot prospects who have trampled on the expectations of Cubs fans so many times that they're understandably wary. So 2003 could be more than the year of Dusty Baker's debut as bench boss, or the season when

Ernie Banks's eternally rosy predictions finally come true (How about: "The Cubs will go on a spree in '03," Ern?).

It also could mark the emergence of a real, genuine, certified center fielder wearing Cubbie blue. Or perhaps not. Patterson's speed—23 stolen bases in 27 attempts—can't overshadow his 189 strikeouts against just 28 walks since he first came up at 21 in 2000.

"I'm still learning the strike zone," the soft-spoken youngster said. "The main thing for me is not to feel the pressure and start changing what got me to the Cubs. Baseball should be fun."

Center of Controversy

Fun was not No. 1 on the agenda for many of Patterson's center field predecessors. They've had some stormy petrels out there, like one of the best, Bill North, who got so fed up with the Cubs' contretemps, on the field and in the front office, that he fled in 1972 to Oakland, teaming with Bert Campaneris to give the A's a one-two leadoff punch that led to their third straight World Series triumph in 1974. A decade later, a new center fielder, Bob "Deer" Dernier, provided the same spark for the Cubs, even though a funny thing happened to that not-quite team of destiny on its way to the 1984 World Series.

Then there was Mel Hall, who always seemed to be seeking—and finding—trouble. He brawled with pitcher Dick Ruthven, another short-tempered Cub, during spring training in 1984, convincing general manager Dallas Green that Hall had to give way to Dernier in the lineup.

So Hall was expendable, becoming part of the fortunate June 15 trade that brought Rick Sutcliffe in from Cleveland to pitch the Cubs to the doorstep of the promised land. On the way out of town, he complained, "Who's this Sutcliffe? I wouldn't mind getting a hit off him." Hall also lamented that the only two Cubs players who didn't hang their heads over lost games were himself and Jay Johnstone, both gone long before the Cubs wrapped up their first-ever NL Eastern Division title. "Why sit around and pout about a loss?"

Jerome Walton, NL Rookie of the Year, was on the center field stage in 1989, helping drive the Cubs to the top in the East Division with a 30-game hitting streak, still the modern-era club record.

"I'll just have to start another one," the cocky freshman said.

But while Walton's ego soared, his performance dipped, and he drifted away in 1992. His wasted potential replayed the saga of Joe "Tarzan" Wallis (1975-79). He preferred to be the center of fans' attention by crashing his motorcycle into various immoveable objects rather than playing center for the Cubs. The resultant bumps and bruises caused the clubhouse whirlpool bath to be renamed the "U.S.S. Wallis," because he spent so much time soaking in it.

The Real Flag Winner

My favorite Cubs center fielder of them all was Rick Monday (1972-76). A solid hitter and a good outfielder, Monday made his most sensational defensive move in Dodger Stadium on April 25, 1976. He swooped down on an American flag, spread on the outfield grass by a couple of political dissidents, just as they lit a match to set it on fire. Monday carried the Stars and Stripes to safety while ballpark cops arrested the intruders and the normally laid-back L.A. crowd rose to give the quick-thinking Cub a standing ovation. "Rick Monday: You Made a Great Play" was the stadium's scoreboard salute, earning him another round of cheers.

"If you want to burn the flag, don't do it in front of me," Monday said. "I've seen too many veterans in hospitals who gave arms and legs for that flag."

Mac Attack

One of the best-hitting Cubs pitchers was Chuck McElroy (1991-93), a chunky southpaw reliever with a good bat and matching attitude.

"I won't see any more fastballs," McElroy predicted after his triple, single and save on the mound ended a Cubs losing streak with a 9-2 Wrigley romp over the Cards on April 11, 1992. "Pitchers have long memories, so they'll throw me curves from now on. I was a pretty good hitter in high school, but I don't care where the Cubs play me as long as I get into the game"

NU, Too, Joe

Joe Girardi dreamed about playing for the Cubs when he was a catcher at Northwestern, a few miles up the road from Wrigley Field. When manager Don Zimmer saw how the rookie handled pitchers in 1989 spring training, he turned that fantasy into reality by keeping him on the roster. Girardi got into that season's playoff with San Francisco, and he thought nothing could top it.

"I was a Cub fan growing up [in Peoria, Illinois], so this still seems unreal," he said.

But that was just a tuneup for Girardi's postseason performances—sadly, no more in Chicago. He made the scene again in Colorado and then earned three World Series rings with the all-conquering Yankees of the 1990s before returning to the Cubs in 2000. Genial Joe took that in stride, because the fans and media appreciated him, even if Sammy Sosa didn't welcome the veteran receiver's advice not to crank up the clubhouse music after the Cubs lost.

CHAPTER 9

Hang Bunting, Not Crepe

The Cubs do not have a "Mr. October" to match Reggie Jackson, who hit three home runs on three consecutive pitches in Game 6 of the 1977 World Series, leading the New York Yankees to a clinching victory over the Los Angeles Dodgers.

In fact, they lurched through the 20th century going pretty much 0 for October as a team. The Cubs did get into the World Series 10 times (1906-07-08, '10, '18, '29, '32, '35, '38 and '45) in a 39-year span, actually winning it twice with back-to-back triumphs over the Detroit Tigers in 1907 and again in 1908.

To paraphrase "The Midnight Ride of Paul Revere," hardly a man is now alive who remembers that famous day and year—October 14, 1908—when Orval Overall gave overall superiority to the Cubs by whitewashing Ty Cobb and the Tigers, 2-0. It wrapped up that World Series in five games. Much, much more significantly, it was the last postseason matchup in close to 100 years that ended with the Cubs winning the final game, at least until the magical, mystical, maybe even miraculous date of October —, 20—?

Fill in the blank yourselves, pennant-hungry Cubs fans. Supply the details from your fevered imaginations, tossing in all those leftover fantasies of an Ernie Banks (or Billy Williams or Ron Santo or Andre Dawson or Sammy Sosa) homer winning the decisive World Series game in Wrigley Field.

Ponder the wild celebrations erupting in Wrigleyville, all over Chicago, throughout Illinois—even in Little Egypt, traditional Cards country—and pretty much around the whole nation, for that matter. You know the legacy of Harry Caray created thousands of closet Cubs fans across North America, Central America and the Carribean islands—heck, just about everywhere the spoken and printed word carried the message of eternal hope that is the essence of Cub fandom.

You're aware that those millions of people are just waiting to join the Wrigley Field regulars in breaking the chain of frustration draped around the Cubs and their loyal supporters for all these years. While you're at it, dream of the final World Series strikeout, fired plateward by Kerry Wood (or, if you prefer, Fergie Jenkins, Ken Holtzman, Rick Reuschel, Rick Sutcliffe, Mark Prior—maybe even Mordecai "Three-Finger" Brown) to vanquish the White Sox and avenge last century's World Series upset by those Hitless Wonders from the South Side.

When it finally happens, Cubs fans will be able to follow Frank Sinatra's marvelous musical advice and put their dreams away for another day. Until that happy day, though, these bittersweet memories will have to tide you over. A glance back at the Cubs playoff series I wrote about years ago—1984, 1989, 1998—turned into an affectionate stroll down memory lane for me. My 1984 book, *Cubs Win!* was a technically, though not totally, accurate title. As we all know, the Cubs were just one game away from the World Series that snake-bitten (or perhaps goat-gored) year, with three grabs at the gold ring, only to hit a stone wall three straight times in San Diego. Summing up that playoff disaster in a single sentence, a broken-hearted Cubs philosopher said of his team's horrendous fold: "It's hard to swing the bat with one hand on your throat."

So, at the dawn of the Dusty Baker era, it might be useful therapy for Cubs fans to join me in looking back, not in anger, but with affectionate nostalgia, at those might-have-been postseason moments. I couldn't help including the summer of 1969 in these reflections, even though the Cubs didn't make the playoffs. That might have been the time when the last of our youthful illusions got swept away under the harsh glare of reality, not just in Wrigley Field, but all over America.

Gary Hits One for Harry

In 1998, the Cubs lost both Harry Caray and Jack Brickhouse, the announcers who made them household words, spreading the legend of Wrigley Field's ivy-covered walls, fun in the sun at the Friendly Confines and finding countless ways to compensate for frustrating seasons. It looked like this one was down the drain, as well, when the Cubs lost an 11-inning September 27 regular-season finale in Houston, 4-3.

They were trudging mournfully off the field, aware that the Giants were on the verge of wrapping up the NL's wild card playoff berth by winning in Colorado.

Then, just like the last-minute stay of execution from the governor in those old movies, the reprieve arrived for the Cubs. It was delivered via a homer by the Rockies' Neifi Perez to beat the Giants, 9-8, putting San Francisco and Chicago in a flat-footed tie at 89-73. The wild card berth was up for grabs in a winner-take-all showdown, and the luck of the draw set the scene in Wrigley Field the following night.

That chilly evening , September 28, 1998, a twice-in-a-lifetime event unfolded on the North Side. Only once before—90 years before, to be exact—had the Cubs been involved in a playoff to make the playoffs.

Gary Gaetti and Steve Trachsel made it a night to remember. Their 1984 and 1989 division-clinching victories took place on the road, so this would be a rare chance for the Cubs to make it happen in their own backyard.

Gaetti, an unlikely late-season pickup from the discard pile, and Trachsel, a prime target for Wrigley boo-birds through much of his up-and-down Cubs tenure, were the unlikely co-heroes in saving a Cubs season that verged perilously close to becoming another of those all-too-familiar late fadeouts. Locked in a wild, three-way struggle with the Giants and New York Mets for the wild card berth throughout August and September, the Cubs went into a tailspin at the end, losing six of their last eight games.

Luckily for them, the Mets had nothing like the finishing kick they found in 1969 to boot the Cubs out of the postseason picture. It was the Giants, counted out with a five-game deficit and just 10 more to play, who made the

Mark Prior displays his amazing potential. Photo courtesy of the Chicago Cubs.

closing charge that would have catapulted them past the Cubs, except for Perez's dramatic home run in Colorado.

"I want to shake that man's hand," Sammy Sosa said of his fellow Dominican Republic import. So did Cubs fans, especially the ones already clutching playoff tickets and pining to see first-round games No. 3 and 4 against Atlanta, scheduled for Wrigley Field on October 3 and 4. At least they got half of their wish, thanks mainly to Trachsel and Gaetti.

"Wrigley Field is always packed and the fans are always making noise, so I didn't feel any extra pressure," Trachsel told me on his way out of the winners' champagne-soaked clubhouse after the traditional bubble bath that follows clinching victories. "If pitchers listen to the crowd instead of concentrating on hitting the catcher's mitt, they're not doing a very good job. But this time, I noticed our fans were yelling for me instead of at me."

From Bleacher Bums to overnight converts in scalped field boxes, the frenzied 39,556 Wrigley customers witnessed mound mastery by Trachsel, who held the Giants hitless for six and one-third innings. His gem gave the Cubs a 2-0 all-time record in such one-game showdowns, with the whole season at stake.

Ironically, both wins knocked the Giants out of the postseason picture, although nine decades and 3,000 miles— the distance between New York and San Francisco— separated these gigantic Cubs-Giants collisions.

The latest one wasn't quite as dramatic—or ferocious— as the replay of a 1908 tied game between the Cubs and the New York Giants that decided the National League pennant.

If Three-Finger Brown hadn't outpitched the immortal Christy Mathewson, 4-2, before a murderously hostile mob in New York's Polo Grounds, the Cubs wouldn't even have been in the 1908 World Series, let alone won it for the last time in the 20th century. All Trachsel's Wrigley Field triumph, 90 years later, gained the Cubs was the right to get swept out of their 1998 first-round NL playoff by the Braves in three straight games.

Regardless, just getting there by beating the Giants, 5-3, to grab that wild card berth gave the Cubs and their fans a badly needed excuse to erupt.

It was Gaetti, the 40-year-old American League refugee, who lit the fuse, breaking up a tense pitching duel between

Trachsel and the Giants' Mark Gardner with a two-run homer in the fifth inning to give the Cubs a lead they never lost. Most of the veteran third baseman's 360 career home runs were stroked for the Minnesota Twins, including one in the 1987 World Series, helping them to topple the St. Louis Cards in a terrific seven-game struggle. Even so, Gaetti never hit a bigger one than the two-run shot he lofted into the left-field bleachers with that 1998 playoff payoff at stake.

"I thought the wind would knock it down," Gaetti said, in between spraying Sammy Sosa and pursuing media minions to douse them with champagne during that wild postgame soak-a-rama in the Cubs' dressing room. Clubhouse mogul Yosh Kawano, who has been doing this for such few and far-between celebrations ever since the 1945 World Series, had his assistants drape lockers with plastic to protect the players' clothes, but anyone with a notebook, microphone or TV camera was fair game.

A religious man, Gaetti credited God for bringing him to Chicago on August 19, his 40th birthday. But the Cards' decision to cut him loose didn't hurt, so the Cubs snapped him up. Nobody, including Gaetti himself, expected him to hit .320 in 37 games down the stretch in 1998, with eight homers and 27 RBIs.

That unexpected punch further down in the batting order took some of the load off Sammy Sosa's back, helping the slugger to ride the whirlwind of 24-hour media demands to probe every aspect of his historic homer derby with Mark McGwire. Gaetti shared the fans' awe over Sosa's 66-homer spree.

"Every time Sammy steps up to the plate, I expect him to hit one out," he said.

Sosa's club-record total, eclipsed that season by McGwire's 70, and again when the Giants' Barry Bonds swatted 73 in 2001, had the fans in hysterics all summer. As the season wore on and the Cubs wore down, it appeared that the Sosa-McGwire circus would be the only game in both towns, with turnstiles spinning merrily at Busch Stadium in St. Louis and at Wrigley to root for this matched set of Paul Bunyan clones.

But the baseball fates wrote a different script. McGwire won the home run battle, only to watch Sosa and the Cubs win the wild card war. And when the Cubs-Giants showdown came down in Wrigley Field, Sosa gratefully turned the hitting hero laurels over to Gaetti and seldom-seen sub Matt Mieske, whose two-run single hiked the home team's edge to 4-0. Sosa later scored on a wild pitch, and that run came in very handy when the Giants launched a desperation ninth-inning rally. Manager Jim Riggleman emptied his bullpen, even tossing starter Kevin Tapani into the fray, but couldn't prevent Bonds from stalking to the plate with the bases loaded, a run across and nobody out. Cubs fans slumped in their seats, anticipating the game-tying grand slam, but lefty reliever Terry Mulholland kept the ball in the park, retiring the southpaw slugger on a sacrifice fly. Closer Rod Beck then touched off jubilation in Wrigleyville by slamming the door on the Giants, preserving Trachsel's 5-3 decision with his 51st save.

Way to Go, Joe

In yet another entry to baseball's endless list of ironic twists, the final San Francisco batter, needing a homer to tie it, instead popped out to end it. Who was that man? Why, none other than Joe Carter, providing a final dividend on the 1984 trade that sent him from the Cubs to Cleveland, bringing Red Baron Rick Sutcliffe here to pilot the Cubs toward their first-ever division title. Along the way, Carter got his own taste of glory, homering off ex-Cub Mitch Williams of the Phillies to win the 1993 World Series for the Toronto Blue Jays. Baseball is, indeed, a funny game.

"What did you expect?" asked first baseman Mark Grace, who caught Carter's game-ending popup. "A 5-0 lead in the ninth inning and we hang on by our fingernails. I guess the Cubs just have to do it that way."

They sure did, although win No. 90 was to be the last one for the 1998 Cubs. They opened the best-of-five playoff series with two losses in Atlanta and closed it by sending rookie sensation Kerry Wood out to duel with his own tender elbow and the Braves' money pitcher, ex-Cub Greg Maddux. Those stacked odds proved impossible to beat, so the Cubs' uphill battle to get into the playoffs ended with a downhill 0-3 slide out of them.

Real Fun at the Old Ballpark

Regardless, '98 was a remarkable, ultra-entertaining roller-coaster ride. Pennant races in both leagues became sideshows, serving as window dressing for the baseball-bashing power struggle between Sosa and McGwire. Those two home run-happy superstars stopped fans from running home, bringing them back to every big-league ballpark, even in the American League, by blowing away residual bitterness from the strike/lockout that had wiped out the 1994 playoffs. That glaring gap in the chain of tradition caused many loyalists to vow they were through with the game that had been a welcome diversion for them.

The backlash hurt the White Sox, who might well have played in the '94 World Series that never was, because many of their fans accused Sox chairman Jerry Reinsdorf of being the behind-the-scenes instigator. Comiskey Park attendance shrank sharply from the all-time high of 2,934,154 in 1991 to 1,391,146 in 1998. In sharp contrast, the Cubs lured 2,623,000 cash customers to their smaller, cozier park in '98, ringing up even higher totals in subsequent seasons.

High Highs, Low Lows

W rigley thrill seekers got their money's worth throughout a zany 1998, right up to the one and only season-ending playoff game. The highest of highs, without a doubt, was Wood's 20-strikeout, one-hit museum piece on May 6. The Astros looked like cardboard cutouts holding toothpicks at the plate while the Cubs right-hander blazed his unhittable assortment past them, winning 2-0.

Perhaps the lowest of lows took place in Milwaukee on September 23. The Cubs had it won when left fielder Brant Brown circled under a fly ball by the Brewers' Geoff Jenkins that should have been the final out of a 7-5 Cub victory. Oops! Whoops! ##%*&##@%&*!!! The elusive horsehide somehow escaped Brown's glove, three runs scored, and the Cubs lost an 8-7 stunner. Ron Santo's visceral shriek of agony from the broadcast booth echoed everywhere Cubs fans huddled around their TV sets and radios.

That ninth-inning blooper could have sounded taps to Cub playoff hopes, and would have, except for Neifi Perez's ninth-inning heroics, four days later in Colorado.

"I forgot about that play before the next game," Brown insisted, forgetting that Cubs fans have memories longer than all the elephants Barnum and Bailey ever assembled under the Big Top. "But everywhere I go, people keep coming up and reminding me about it."

Game 1: Tomahawked

So the rejuvenated Cubs headed to the sunny South, intending to make the most of sneaking into the postseason picture. They wasted little time making the least of it. In the box score, this 7-1 playoff-opening loss to the Braves on September 30 looks like a rout. Yet the familiar might-have-been chorus started even earlier than usual for the Cubs, with their postseason history overburdened by such regrets. With two out and nobody on in the second inning, shortstop Jose Hernandez muffed Andruw Jones's grounder, and Michael Tucker, destined for a brief stay with the Cubs in 2001, promptly homered off loser Mark Clark. That was all John Smoltz, tough as a starter before he became Atlanta's virtually unhittable closer, needed to put his team into sweep mode.

Game 2: Tap Trapped

Three words sum up this 2-1 heartbreaker—tough luck, Tap. A 19-game regular-season winner, the veteran right-hander deserved his 20th on Oct. 1 in Turner Field, but didn't get it. Working on a four-hit shutout and nursing a 1-0 lead with one out in the ninth inning, Tapani served up a game-tying homer to Javy Lopez. The Braves pushed over a run off reliever Terry Mulholland in the 10th, putting a stranglehold on the best-of-five series.

Eternal optimist Sammy Sosa refused to concede.

"It's not the end of the world," said Sammy, who would finish the series homerless, just two for 11. "My [congratulatory] call from the president is on hold, but if we win that first game at home, things could change."

Game 3: Strike Three

Things didn't change. Greg Maddux bested Kerry Wood, 6-2, on October 3 in Wrigley Field to go 8-1 lifetime against his former team. The Cubs batted a puny .181 in the series, wasting good starts by Clark, Tapani and Wood. Gaetti, hero of the playoff to get into the playoffs, was a bust in the real thing, contributing a single in 11 trips.

"How about two grand slams [both by the Braves] and a wide strike zone?" Gaetti summed up the series, adding a sly jab at plate umpires' calls, which the Cubs felt favored Atlanta's pitchers throughout.

Sammy Gets Kicks on Homer Route 66

Wherever Sammy Sosa and Mark McGwire went in September 1998, adoring fans, TV cameras and nosy newspaper types were sure to go. Sosa had been getting the superstar treatment ever since his phenomenal power surge in June, when he hit an unprecedented 20 home runs. On the road, the media crush grew so demanding that Sosa had to meet separately with them before the first game of every series.

As successful at public relations as he was at the plate, Sammy had been briefed about Hack Wilson's club-record 56 homers for the Cubs in 1930. When Sosa slammed No. 57 to better Hack on September 4 in Pittsburgh, he paid proper respects to the historical significance of Wilson's—and his—feats. Precisely because he made himself available while the Cards' McGwire ducked the spotlight whenever he could, Sosa found himself living in a fishbowl. The genial slugger seemed to thrive on it, especially the Dominican flags frenziedly waved by his backers in every ballpark.

"McGwire's the man in this country," was Sosa's stock answer about those emotional scenes. "In the Dominican Republic, I'm the man."

Before both candidates for The Man from Everywhere collided in St. Louis on September 7-8, their last head-to-head meeting of the season, McGwire tried some diplomacy of his own, predicting their great home run chase would end in a deadlock. Then the St. Louis muscleman let his feats outstrip his speeches, homering in each game to equal Roger Maris's single-season record of 61 on Monday afternoon and surpassing it Tuesday night with No. 62, a low liner off Steve Trachsel that just cleared Busch Stadium's left-field barrier.

Just like the hysteria that erupted in Cincinnati when Pete Rose singled to break Ty Cobb's all-time mark of 4,191 hits, fireworks signaled the start of a prolonged salute to McGwire by St. Louis fans. Sosa exchanged hugs with his rival for the title of New Sultan of Swat, but their race went on, right down to the season's final days. By the time Sosa stroked a pair of Wrigley Field homers to top Maris's record on September 13, helping the Cubs to beat the Brewers, 11-10, there was hardly a dry eye in the packed house, including Sammy's.

"I was crying a little, but it was for my family and these Chicago fans," Sosa said. "I wanted to hit home runs today as a present to them."

The next day, Sosa touched all the bases off the field, telling the media in San Diego that President Bill Clinton had called to congratulate him and wish the Cubs luck in their playoff quest. Battling a slump and concerned about hurricane damage to his Carribean homeland, Sosa broke out of it, actually grabbing a brief one-homer edge over McGwire on September 25 with No. 66, a towering blast in Houston's Astrodome. But that was it for Sosa, and McGwire roared past him again, adding five more home runs for an even 70, a standard that lasted only three seasons, until Barry Bonds's 73 rewrote baseball history.

"When other guys help us win, it's better for the Cubs," Sosa said. "What's good for the Cubs works for me."

1989: A Giant Setback

This was the season of something else. The Cubs did not play their normal game, station-to-station baseball, waiting for Ernie Banks or Dave Kingman or Leon Durham or somebody—anybody—to play longball. Their faithful fans, longing for some playoff ball, had seen their hopes implode under the weight of a collapsing team and a choking manager (Leo Durocher) on the doorstep of the 1969 playoffs.

Then, when the 1984 Cubs finally finished first, in the NL's Eastern Division, at least, they proved not to be the beasts of the East. Chicago was confident that the end of the Cubs' self-imposed 39-year postseason boycott also would end their run of 76 years (since 1908) without a World Series triumph. The emotional scars from their traumatic 1984 playoff choke-a-thon in San Diego still hung around Wrigley Field like Banquo's ghost when the 1989 Cubs got going with an old outlook, installed by a new manager.

The old approach was new to the Cubs, even if Don Zimmer wasn't. Their second-year field boss, an old-school guy, gave them a totally new blueprint in spring training: Whatever it takes to score a run, do it. The Cubs did it, to the surprise and delight of Cubs fans everywhere. They won their second NL East title in five years by duplicating the previous season's .261 team batting average and getting much more production out of those league-leading 1,438 hits. Their 702 runs, also tops in the NL, gave the main starters—Greg Maddux, Rick Sutcliffe, Mike Bielecki, Scott Sanderson—enough cushion to pile up a combined 64 wins—19 by Maddux.

Throw in 36 saves by Mitch "Wild Thing" Williams, with Les Lancaster and Paul Assenmacher combining for 14 more. Jerome Walton and Dwight Smith finished 1-2 in NL Rookie of the Year voting, and Ryne Sandberg was the power guy with 30 homers, Andre Dawson adding 21 more. It computed to a 93-69 record, six satisfying lengths ahead of those 1969 villains, the New York Mets.

S.F. WILL Prevail

So the NL playoff between the Cubs and San Francisco Giants, the West champs, should have been a dead-even slugfest throughout the best-of-seven series. After all, the Cubs and Giants fought to a 6-6 draw in the regular season, each team going 3-3 in windblown Wrigley Field and even windier Candlestick Park. The Cubs figured to have an edge in starting pitchers, but the Giants boasted their "Pacific Sock Exchange," left fielder Kevin Mitchell and first baseman Will Clark, a potent pair, powering up in '89 to produce 70 homers and 236 RBI. The last thing anyone expected was a decisive first-sacker sock duel between Clark and Mark Grace of the Cubs. Clark won it by a sliver, batting .650 on 13 for 20 to Grace's .647 on 11 for 17, but San Francisco took the series and the NL pennant by a margin wider than the Golden Gate Bridge, breezing home in five games.

Game 1: Clark's Park

Will Clark grabbed the Cubs by the throat immediately and never let go. Behind his booming bat, the Giants shocked a wildly confident overflow Wrigley Field throng of 39,195 to romp, 11-3, in the all-important series opener. Greg Maddux made the first of his two ineffective starts, with the Cubs' ace getting trumped—and clubbed.

Game 2: Rick Rocked

The Cubs pounded their longtime mound mainstay, Rick Reuschel, for a half-dozen runs in the first inning, convincing worried fans that they would be back from the upcoming three games in San Francisco with this series still on the line and the NL pennant up for grabs. The Giants refused to lie down and die, though, making it uncomfortably close before the home team won, 9-5.

Game 3: Cubs "Robbed"

The sight of pitcher Dave Dravecky, who broke his arm making a delivery when he returned from surgery to remove a cancerous tumor, was enough to fire up a Candlestick crowd of 62,065. The Giants got the emotional lift they needed from Robby Thompson's two-run homer in the seventh inning, just enough to nip the Cubs, 5-4. In yet another of those bizarre playoff twists that seem to bedevil the North Siders, reliever Les Lancaster lost track of the count, believing it was three and 0, so he grooved a fastball to Thompson, who whacked it over the left field wall.

"Anybody can make a mistake," Lancaster lamented. "I looked at the scoreboard, and it said 3-0. I didn't want to walk Thompson, so I threw a strike."

Game 4: Greg's Dregs

With everything on the line, manager Don Zimmer had no option other than starting Maddux with three days' rest. Once again, the young right-hander couldn't get the job done, so the Cubs sank into a hopeless 3-1 series deficit. This 6-4 loss got pinned on reliever Steve Wilson, but it closed out Maddux's undistinguished postseason log for the Cubs with an 0-1 record and an embarrassing 13.50 ERA.

Game 5: Rick's Revenge

With Reuschel's second start standing between them and elimination, the Cubs couldn't leap the hurdle of the chubby veteran's pinpoint control. Still, they led 2-1 until—guess who?—Clark's clutch two-run single made the difference in a 3-2 squeaker, propelling the Giants into the World Series and sending the Cubs home with their sixth straight playoff road loss.

My mind flashed back more than 25 years, to when I watched the Leo Durocher era end with an orgy of Cub self-destruction. In 1972, a chubby rookie joined the team, to be joined three years later by his brother, Paul. A quiet, strapping farm boy from downstate Illinois, Rick stuck around to win 135 games for the Cubs, but had to go to both coasts for the crowning World Series experience—with the Yankees in 1981 and the '89 Giants—that eluded so many Chicago players on both sides of town.

Cubs Roar in '84

B lithely oblivious of the playoff fate awaiting them, the Cubs staged a hit (and pitch) show all season. They were a likeable bunch of guys, with handsome young catcher Jody Davis ("Jo-dee! Jo-dee!" bellowed the second-generation Bleacher Bums) reprising Randy "Rebel" Hundley's 1969 role as Wrigley's fan favorite. Of course, things had changed in those 15 years, so the Confederate flags that fluttered from the bleachers when Hundley came to bat were long gone by then. But Gary "Sarge" Matthews, Sr., provided both charisma and punch that year, unaware that he would follow his son's footsteps back to Chicago, joining Dusty Baker's coaching staff in 2003, two years after Gary, Jr., left the Cubs to start living up to his potential in Pittsburgh. Bob "Deer" Dernier and Ryne "Baby Ruth" Sandberg swiped a combined 77 bases at the top of the order, while Ron "Penguin" Cey (25) and Leon "Bull" Durham (23) were the homer heroes, with Red Baron Sutcliffe (16-1 after the trade), Steve "Rainbow" Trout (13-7) and Dennis "Eck" Eckersley (10-8) as the double-digit starters.

Closer Lee Smith (9-7 record, 33 saves) should have been nicknamed "Mr. Bullpen," so Green and manager Jim Frey doubtless felt unloading Willie Hernandez would not weaken the relief corps. What happened during the '84 playoff proved them wrong, especially when the smoke cleared from that gut-wrenching Game 5 in San Diego.

Green Light Turns Red

On the field, everything went well—hell, went perfectly—for the 1984 Cubs. Off the field, they probably lost their first-round playoff a year before it started. Sure, general manager Dallas Green gave the green light to grabbing ace Rick Sutcliffe on June 13, 1984, in a blockbuster deal with Cleveland. The Red Baron pitched the Cubs into the postseason, but an earlier move by Green could have been the one that tossed them out of it.

On May 22, 1983, the Cubs dealt lefty reliever Willie Hernandez to the Phillies, who compounded Green's goof by letting a pitcher they deemed expendable get away to the Detroit Tigers. Both teams soon regretted that choice, though it turned out to be much more costly for the Cubs.

"I told Willie this would be his last Cub contract unless he buckled down," Green warned. "He was wasting his ability."

True, Hernandez was no Rollie Fingers or Bruce Sutter in his Chicago tenure (1977-83), and no Kenny Holtzman as a starter, either, despite his baffling screwball, hard to hit from either side of the plate.

"They tried to fool people by saying I had a bad attitude," Hernandez told me when I asked why a left-handed reliever

*It's champagne-spraying time for catcher Jody Davis (left) and
pitcher Rick Sutcliffe after the division-clinching triumph in
Pittsburgh. Framed in the middle is longtime Cubs broadcaster
Jack Brickhouse.*

with such explosive stuff had been sent down to the minors
by the Cubs.

Manager Sparky Anderson thought Hernandez's attitude
was terrific in 1984, when the Tiger closer's bullpen
dominance helped the Tigers win 104 games and breeze
into the World Series against the San Diego Padres. So
Hernandez was sitting at home, watching the Cubs blow
their NL playoff to those same, highly beatable Padres.
Privately, he admitted it would have been more fun to face
his old teammates.

Instead, the southpaw saved Game 3 and did it again in the clinching fifth game, while the Tigers clawed the Padres to wrap up this World Series mismatch.

"Do I feel sorry for the Cubs?" Hernandez mulled the often-answered question. "There are some good guys over there, but I don't dwell on the past."

Ryne's So Fine

Ryne Sandberg should make the Hall of Fame sooner rather than later. If the voters who figured Ryno wasn't worthy enough to make it in 2003, his first year of eligibility, had been in Wrigley Field on June 23, 1984, the clutch-clouting Cubs second baseman might have been a unanimous first-ballot pick. That's an afternoon right up there with May 12, 1970 (Ernie Banks's 500th home run) or September 13, 1988 (Sammy Sosa's historic 61st and 62nd homers) in the hearts, minds and memories of Cubs fans.

Sandberg slammed back-to-back homers off his former teammate, Cards relief ace Bruce Sutter, to bring the Cubs back from the brink of defeat in the ninth inning and again in the 10th. The 12-11 Cubs comeback, nationally televised as NBC's *Game of the Week*, became the Ryne Sandberg Show, a showcase for the Quiet Man's five for six and seven RBI.

"I'm in a state of shock," Sandberg confessed after his career day.

The Immaculate Deflection

S o were Cubs fans, slowly realizing this team was for
real, even if Sandberg's heroics seemed unreal. For
those who weren't totally convinced, what happened on
August 2 swept away the last shred of doubt.

With the Cubs clinging to a 3-2 edge over Montreal in
the ninth inning, one out and runners on first and third,
the Wrigley crowd of 22,485 wriggled nervously, because
Pete Rose, one of the all-time clutch hitters, faced Lee Smith.
Sure enough, Rose rocketed a liner up the middle, ticketed
for the game-tying single.

Whoops! Somehow, Smith's self-defensive glove stab
deflected the ball off his shoulder, straight to shortstop Dave
Owen, who turned it into the game-ending double play.
Even Harry Caray's jubilant "Holy Cow!" came out as a
hoarse croak after that quasi-divine stroke of luck.

"The Cubs are destined, I guess," shrugged Expos pitcher
Bryn Smith.

California Cubquake

T he 1984 Cubs were a team of destiny, all right.
Sadly, it wasn't the one their fans had in mind—a
rendezvous, not with destiny, but a rematch of their 1945
World Series against the Detroit Tigers, ending in satisfying
revenge for that seven-game bashing by the Bengals. After
the Cubs won the first two games of their National League
championship series, there was no way they could go to San
Diego and lose three straight times. Supremely confident

Chicagoans snapped up every available ticket, enabling scalpers to demand—and get—up to $1,000 for good, not great, seats.

Pent-up hysteria on the North Side turned into absolute assurance when the Cubs blew away the overmatched Padres, 13-0 and 4-2 on October 2 and 3, for a 2-0 stranglehold on this one-sided playoff.

Or so it seemed, even to the losers, who admitted some of them huddled on the flight back to San Diego to plan hunting trips and vacations as soon as the Cubs polished them off. But not all of them quit.

"When we got off that plane, we were dead," Padres Hall of Famer Tony Gwynn told me years later. "Somehow, all that changed when we won the first game at home. Even when we fell behind Sutcliffe [in the decisive Game 5], I knew we'd get to him."

They did.

Paradise Lost

No better way to explain it than that *Chicago Tribune* headline on October 8, 1984. It was the morning after, but the hangover wouldn't go away. Even after the last Cubs fan, player or official who suffered through that Gloomy Sunday is gone, it will hang around, like wisps of fog over Wrigley Field's scoreboard.

The Cubs led 3-0 in the sixth inning and 3-2, with six-foot-seven Sutcliffe visibly shrinking from fatigue, when the Padres came to bat in the seventh. Frey stuck with his valiant bearded giant too long, then brought in Trout, too late. An agonizing error by first baseman Durham and a bad hop on

Gwynn's wicked grounder off Sandberg's shoulder at second base turned the game, the season and the Cubs' World Series fantasy into confetti, blowing away in Chicago's bitter winter winds.

Maybe, just maybe, it wouldn't have happened if Willie Hernandez had been there in the Cubs' bullpen, ready to douse that seventh-inning fire. Larry Bowa was at shortstop that day when the last echo of that season's hit song ("We'll keep 'em flyin' high for Cubbie Blue") faded away, just like the Cubs. Bowa was a Seattle Mariners coach in 2000 when we recalled the '84 Cubs' demise, just before the Mariners faced the White Sox in a Comiskey Park playoff opener.

"Chicago sure was a Cubs town that year," Bowa said. "Too bad we couldn't give their fans what they deserved."

1969: Still on Our Minds

The Cubs didn't make the playoffs in 1969. All they did was make believers out of their fans, and then break their hearts. Maybe the words of Ernie Banks, Mr. Cub then and always, can turn those memories of a sour September back toward the way it was in that fun-filled summer.

"The thing that makes 1969 stand out in my mind was our closeness, just like the neighborhood guys hanging out together," Banks said. "It was a happening in Wrigley Field."

Maybe, one of these years—or centuries—it'll happen again.

CHAPTER 10

They Put the Wriggle in Wrigleyville

The Wrigley family gave the Cubs much more than a name for their ballpark. The Wrigley way of operating left an indelible mark on Chicago's National League franchise, on the players and managers who wore Cub uniforms, and especially on the front-office people entrusted to put a product on the field.

Judging the Wrigley era and its aftermath as an utter failure, solely by the won-lost record, the yearly standings, and the team's late-season tendency to fold up like a Murphy bed would be easy. Too easy. It is true that the Cubs took the field in 2003 with a depressing legacy—one World Series (1945) appearance in the last 64 years, going all the way back to 1939. The year before that, they got into the Series, and lost. Ditto for their World Series forays in 1935, '32 (the year of Babe Ruth's legendary called-shot homer in Wrigley Field), '29, '18 and '10. Only the last five (1929 through 1945) came on the Wrigley watch, because William Wrigley, Jr., did not buy controlling interest in the Cubs until 1919.

Regardless, a lot of easy laughs about the way their team always seemed to gum up the works marred the legacy of these chewing gum tycoons. It was unavoidable, since Wrigley's Spearmint met the payroll for decades. Despite that, Wrigley Field's blend of day baseball, the cozy confines that enabled fans to see their favorite player's five o'clock shadow sprout in the later innings and the el trains, buses and trolleys (in the early decades), depositing a new crop of young fans on the doorstep every season, created generations of lifelong Cubs fans. Once they got hooked on sunshine, the outfield ivy and the irrepressible optimism of Ernie Banks, rooting for the Cubs became a terminal disease, with no known cure.

But there was a lot more to it than that. Perhaps if the Cubs had been owned by robber barons instead of the Wrigleys, a George Steinbrenner clone would have bought the team. In that case, Cubs fans feared the new owner's first priorities might be: (1) Tear down Wrigley Field; (2) Turn the Cubs into the Midwest Yankees after transplanting them into some shiny, sterile, suburban stadium, with lots of skyboxes and garish, profitable ads on the outfield walls; (3) Sign hordes of boring, overpaid mercenaries to win the pennant and World Series every year.

Maybe such draconian solutions would satisfy the win-or-else mentality that's changed sports all over America, substituting ferocity for fun at the old ballpark, Little League field or anywhere else the outcome is more important than

*A real slice of Cubs history comes together in 1962 when hands-
on owner Phil Wrigley (center) greets players Don Elston, Billy
Williams and Glen Hobbie (left), along with George Altman,
Ernie Banks and Bob Will (right).*

the game itself. It wouldn't be the way I want to go, along
with what I suspect is a shrinking minority of old-time
diehard Cubs fans. One man who wanted the Cubs to win,
but would not bend the rules to make it happen, was Philip
Knight Wrigley. He inherited the leadership—and the
burden—of the Cubs when his father, William Wrigley, Jr.,
died in 1932. What P. K. didn't know about baseball was
just about everything, though he struggled manfully to carry
on the family's hobby-business, with occasional success amid
frequent, scatter-brained experiments.

Phil's His Phone Man

A gentle man and a gentleman, Wrigley was uncomfortable in the spotlight and incapable of being a hands-on owner in the daily operation of the Cubs. He much preferred to tinker with old cars in the garage of his Lake Geneva, Wisconsin, mansion and spend time with his wife, Helen, and their children.

In the meantime, P. K. answered his own telephone, taking calls on his listed number and patiently explaining to fans why the Cubs had gone straight downhill since that last pennant in 1945. He didn't snub the writers, either. I know, because I had several phone chats with Wrigley during the turbulent Leo Durocher era that turned into page one stories in the *Chicago Tribune's* sports section.

Regardless of his ownership skills, or lack thereof, this unconventional Cubs boss—as far removed from the bombastic style of Yankees dictator George Steinbrenner as Mohandas K. Ghandi was from Blood and Guts Patton—frequently got a pass from Chicago fans and media alike. His old-fashioned decency and genuine concern for Wrigley Field and the comfort and convenience of Cubs fans overshadowed some of his bizarre brainstorms. The blue ribbon for such tomfoolery got pinned on the 1961-65 revolving College of Coaches, which quickly turned into hilarious, back-stabbing burlesque. A close second was Wrigley's hard-to figure hiring of former U.S. Air Force Lt. Colonel Bob Whitlow as "athletic director" of the Cubs, a 1963-65 experiment that produced nothing except more front-office confusion.

Ernie Who?

E ven what most people credited as the crowning moment of the Wrigley regime—the 1953 signing of a slender, 22-year-old shortstop from the Kansas City Monarchs—was something of a surprise to P. K.

"Why did you pay $35,000 to bring in Ernie Banks?" Wrigley asked his general manager, Wid Matthews.

"Other teams are after him," Matthews said of the youngster who became the Cubs' second black player, with second baseman Gene Baker already under contract. "Anyway, we need a roommate for Baker."

The Wrigley Papers

L eo Durocher's fifteen minutes of fame on the Chicago sporting scene actually lasted for more than seven years (1966-72). The fun times under his managerial reign zipped by quickly, but when the S.S. Durocher hit that 1969 iceberg, cleverly disguised as the New York Mets, and began to sink, Cubs fans stood by on deck for what seemed like an eternity. So did Wrigley, a very loyal man, who stuck with his embattled skipper until the waves of discontent washed away all hope of salvation. Even then, P. K. went down with guns blazing. His famous full-page newspaper ad of September 3, 1971, totally backed Durocher, unlike the traditional front-office "vote of confidence," the kiss of death that signals the manager of a struggling team to start packing his bags, send the wife and kids back to their hometown and scan the want ads.

"Durocher Dumpers" Dumped On

Wrigley's plain-spoken case for keeping Durocher on the job caused a media sensation. Cubs fans, many still in mourning over the way the 1969 dream season ended in a nightmare, seemed evenly divided in the great stay-or-go debate. At least nobody doubted where P. K. stood. Some excerpts from his unique manifesto, which *Tribune* sports editor Cooper Rollow dubbed "The Wrigley Papers:"

TO ALL CUBS FANS AND ANYBODY ELSE WHO IS INTERESTED

"The Cub organization is at sixes and sevens and somebody has to do something. The responsibility falls on me. By tradition, this would call for a press conference, following which there would be as many versions of what I had to say as there were reporters present.

"For a quarter of a century, the Cubs were perennial dwellers of the second division in spite of everything we could think of and try—experienced managers, inexperienced managers, rotating managers, no manager, but revolving coaches—we were still there in the also-rans. We settled on Leo Durocher, who had the knowledge to build a contender and win pennants, also knowing he has always been a controversial figure, because he was never cut out to be a diplomat.

"This year there has been a constant campaign to dump Durocher that has even affected the players. After careful consideration, Leo is the team manager and the 'Dump Durocher Clique' might as well give up. He is running the team and if some of the players lie down on the job, we will see what we can do to find them happier homes."

Phil Wrigley, president, Chicago National League ball club.

"P.S. If only we could find more team players like Ernie Banks."

Wrigley's unprecedented move—stating his case with paid, full-page ads in all four Chicago newspapers—produced predictably strong reactions. After all, this was no Mike Ditka, creating daily headlines by manipulating the media with his staged tantrums. When Philip K. Wrigley came out of his self-imposed isolation to tell off pouting Cubs players, grumbling Cubs fans and sharply critical media, they all had something to say about it.

Fergie Fires Back

"It's a bunch of junk," Ferguson Jenkins, ace of the Cub pitching staff, said of Wrigley's blast. Milt Pappas, the Cubs' player representative, who almost exactly a year later was to hurl a Wrigley Field no-hitter that missed being a perfect game on one borderline call, was equally disturbed.

"This stuff is getting out of hand," Pappas said of the uproar swirling around the team ever since a stormy meeting on August 23 between Durocher and unhappy Cubs players. "It's a joke, and every day things get worse."

Some Cubs, fearing they were the ones Wrigley had been aiming at, fired back with anonymous barbs.

"Durocher's not the only problem," one said. "This guy [Wrigley] has done some unbelievable things. It's a sick situation."

Another player added, "Durocher gives us all kinds of hell, but he never told anybody he was laying down."

Early Warning Unheeded

A lot of this yes-you-did, no-you-didn't kid stuff could have been avoided if the Cubs had listened to Wrigley's warning, a few days after that infamous clubhouse shouting match. I called him at his Lake Geneva home on August 26, 1971, and he didn't mince words.

"We're not playing ball," he said of the fading, quarreling Cubs. "Twenty-five years ago, I'd have gone into the clubhouse and told them myself, but I'm getting too old for that. I'll talk to Ron Santo and Ernie Banks in my [Wrigley Building] office and hope they get the message to the other players. They owe it to Cubs fans to stop piling fuel on the fire. It doesn't matter if they don't like the manager or me or anyone else."

The Cubs were six games behind East Division leader Pittsburgh when Wrigley spoke with me. By the time his full-page ad came out, a week later, the gap had grown to nine games, and the Cubs were out of the race. Soon after the season ended, Wrigley gave Durocher a one-year contract, also signing Banks as a coach at the end of his brilliant career. It simply delayed the inevitable. When the Cubs floundered early in 1972, Durocher got fired, but putting a revolving door on the manager's office in Wrigley Field didn't produce many miracles. Dusty Baker arrived in 2003, the 20th manager in the 30 years since Leo exited, with the Cubs still chasing the Wrigley Word Series that had eluded them since 1945.

The Tribune Times

The Cubs made threatening gestures here and there throughout the 1970s, the last decade of Wrigley family ownership, never quite getting over the hump. It really was the end of an era when Phil Wrigley died at 82 on April 12, 1977. His wife inherited the estate, including the gum company and the Cubs, but she passed away soon after. That put a tremendous inheritance tax burden on the family, so selling the baseball team was a solution to easing the debt and keeping the Wrigley family business afloat.

The new owner, Bill Wrigley, found a willing buyer at a bargain basement price. The Tribune Company, owner of flagship properties in the *Chicago Tribune* and WGN, plus newspapers, radio and TV stations, along with other enterprises throughout North America, snapped up the Cubs on June 16, 1981, for close to $21 million, plus an option on the valuable land under Wrigley Field.

Green Light for Dallas

Trib brass made a smart move by luring a savvy executive, Andy McKenna, from the White Sox to take over as Cubs president. McKenna, a behind-the-scenes power in Chicago business, sports and social circles, had the clout to get things done. He got everybody's attention in a hurry by hiring Dallas Green on October 15, 1981, as general manager, with broad authority to remake the organization and rebuild the Cubs into contenders. And as soon as he left Philadelphia to travel to Chicago with a whip and a chair, Green began making waves.

A big, bluff, imposing man with a booming voice, Green liked the spotlight and loved baseball. Born in Delaware, he made the short move to Philadelphia for a 26-year hitch with the Phillies, doing it all, from farmhand to fringe pitcher (20-22 lifetime) to the front office to back to the dugout as manager of the 1980 world champions. His Phils won that World Series from the Kansas City Royals, managed by Jim Frey. Just four years later, Green and Frey teamed up to take the Cubs to the brink of the 1984 World Series—but no closer.

Green and Bear It

B ut getting the Cubs that far created some extraordinary stretches of controversy, in-fighting, bluster and bumps in the road, including the firing in 1983 of Lee Elia, Green's personal choice as manager. One thing Green promised—and lived up to—was that he would never duck a fight. The hard-driving boss found himself in plenty of them throughout his stormy six seasons in Chicago. While I was writing *Cubs Win!* in 1984, with the city, the state and much of America (thanks to Harry Caray's charisma) frothing at the mouth over the prospect of this downtrodden team actually in the playoffs, I sat down with Dallas in his office to get his state of the franchise update. As always, he was frank, open and emotional in describing what the GM (with some justification) viewed as a personal triumph over the resistance to the sweeping changes he labeled "Building a New Tradition." Wrigley Field traditionalists didn't like some of Green's moves, even objecting when he painted that slogan on the park's outside wall at Clark and Addison. That got his dander up, so he cut loose with gusto.

"Cubs fans were used to rooting for losing teams," he said. "That's unacceptable to me. I heard people complaining that 71-91 [the record in 1983, Green's second season as Cub commander] made our New Tradition seem like the same old stuff. The Cubs were trying to rebuild with trades, but the emphasis should be on player development and scouting. That calls for patience."

Out of the Frey Pan

But when the Cubs blew three straight playoff games in 1984, it was no choking matter. Green followed that with two crucial mistakes—hiring Gene Michael as manager after Jim Frey got fired in 1986 and bringing Michael back for one more losing season. Green's solution was to hire himself as manager, but he changed his mind in 1987 and went back home to Philadelphia, taking the tattered remnants of the New Tradition with him. If you're scoring at home, Green departed with one winning season, one division title, one traumatic playoff collapse (all of that in 1984) and an overall 463-504 record for his six years on the job.

Of all the million might-have-beens in Cubs history, that 0-3 postseason punishment by the Padres has been postmortemed almost as much as September, 1969, when the front-running Cubs got blind-sided by the onrushing Mets. If the Cubs had won any of those three games in San Diego, bringing a World Series to Wrigley Field for the first time in 39 years, Green could have been elected mayor of Chicago, or at least the alderman for Wrigleyville's 44th Ward. Instead, he became a footnote in Cubs history, albeit a highly entertaining one. Unhappy about what he considered uninformed interference by Tribune Company brass, Green still appreciated the irony of the situation.

"We had the Padres by the throat, and we didn't squeeze them one more time," he said. "That's why I didn't get the time I needed to start getting a steady flow of youngsters from the farm system. That's baseball. You win or you're out."

The Jim and Zim Show

So the torch got passed to Jim Frey, another spin of the merry-go-round that assures baseball's front offices a steady supply of the same old faces, recycled into new jobs. It's the way the Good Ole Boys network works. Cubs fans weren't surprised when Frey stepped into the executive suite and tapped his boyhood chum, Don Zimmer, to complete the 1986-87 managerial switcheroo from Frey to John Vukovich to Michael to Frank Lucchesi in a bewildering who's-minding-the-store-today? sequence. Frey's four seasons as general manager also matched Green's lone division title and playoff loss, but little else to arouse Cubs fans from their lethargy.

They went into the 1990s with high hopes, inflated by an upbeat '89 showing. Overinflated, as it turned out. The

Cubs displayed an inspired brand of baseball, becoming the Boys of Zimmer for that fun-filled campaign, but, like 1984, it was a one-shot deal. They were all shot in 1990. Zimmer was gone early in the next season, followed by Frey when it ended. Most of Frey's tenure was spent on the phone, in valiant efforts to trade for enough pitching to fill the void caused by Rick Sutcliff's plethora of injuries. The record shows his pleas went mainly unheeded.

"Other teams look at the standings, and when they see you're in trouble, their price for a trade goes out of sight," Frey grumbled. "I'm trying to get a relief pitcher to shore up the bullpen, they want a Mark Grace or a Greg Maddux in return."

Cubs Lose Greg, the Golden Egg

The emergence of young right-hander Maddux could have given the Cubs a building block for the decade, although that dream evaporated when the 1992 NL Cy Young Award winner fled to Atlanta after a 20-11 record for the fourth-place Cubs that season. At least that defection did not happen on Frey's watch. Even though they couldn't get to the .500 mark in 1991-92, his last turns as general manager, there was plenty of talent on the Cubs' roster at the decade's outset. In his prime, Ryne Sandberg swatted 40 homers in 1991, topping the NL and becoming the only second baseman to lead the league since 1925, when Hall of Famer Rogers Hornsby hit 39.

Mark Grace was settling in for a long run at first base, piling up hits at a pace that would produce more (1,754) than any other big-leaguer in the 1990s. The fancy fielder also earned his keep by scooping shortstop Shawon Dunston's throws out of the dirt. And Andre Dawson, warming up right field bleacherites for the hero worship they soon would lavish on Sammy Sosa, paced the Cubs with a .310 average and 27 homers, closely tailed by Grace (.309) and Sandberg (.306). Cub nostalgia buffs noted approvingly that it was the first time three regulars batted over .300 since 1945 (NL batting king Phil Cavarretta, .355; Smilin' Stan Hack, .325; Don Johnson, .302). Regardless, all that potential and performance couldn't save Frey's job. With all the talent he left behind, the Cubs could be, might, be...weren't consistent contenders for the rest of the 20th century.

The Times of Himes

What happened? In an era of skyrocketing salaries, the Cubs couldn't—or wouldn't—keep pace, at the pay window and in the standings, so the 1990s produced a familiar, i.e. sad, scenario. The movers and shakers in the *Chicago Tribune's* ivory tower understandably wanted to turn the page, breaking away from the Wrigley era of front-office futility and inability to win consistently. They sought no more insider general managers like John Holland (1957-75), P. K. Wrigley's consigliore for a generation of Cubs ups and downs—mostly downs. Or the caretaker regime of E. R. "Salty" Saltwell (1976), the longtime manager of Wrigley Field operations, who actually filled the GM chair for that season. Bob Verdi, the quick-witted *Tribune* columnist, penned the perfect description of Saltwell's brief sojourn: "Salty has gone from counting hot dogs to signing them."

And no more revolving College of Coaches fiascos (1961-65), either. True, Andy McKenna's first foray to other, presumably greener, pastures for outsider Dallas Green did not end well; likewise for Jim Frey's twin terms as manager and GM.

Here Comes Sammy

S o the owners went to the other end of town at the end of the 1991 season, bringing in Larry Himes from the White Sox to run the show. For some outraged Cubs fans, they might as well have gone to the ends of the earth. Himes sought to silence his critics by proving he was a man of action. Even better, decisive action, something virtually unheard of in sleepy Cubs lagoons, at least since Green fled in disgust.

"It all comes down to pitching," was the first public utterance by Himes when he took the Cubs' reins on November 14, 1991, skipping the usual glad-to-be-here pleasantries. That was typical of Himes's brusque approach. A man who knew his baseball, he was sorely in need of a charisma transplant. His lack of charm rankled the media, making it more imperative for Himes to produce a Cubs contender.

"That's a nice speculation, but it's nonsense," was his way of denying that the decision to let popular Cubs outfielder Andre Dawson go after 1992 was a payroll-slashing move. Of course it was, but Himes already had rolled the dice on a move that still has profound effects on the Cubs and their fans, not to mention baseball history, more than a decade later. On March 30, 1992, the Cubs traded veteran slugger George Bell to the White Sox for the raw potential of 23-year-old Sammy Sosa, along with pitcher Ken Patterson.

The blockbuster deal created tidal waves of pro and con on both sides of town. This early reaction from a Cubs beat writer was typical:

"I hate to say I told you so, but I told you so. Bell for Sosa was a bad trade the day it was made, and it looks worse every day. Bell instigated most of the clubhouse horseplay. Without him, Shawon Dunston has become the quietest man there. It's clear Himes wants to tear up the Cubs and rebuild. The Cubs don't need to be torn up. Himes should know there are no five-year plans with this ownership. If the GM doesn't produce fast, he's gone."

Can't Repeat Sox-cess

With a three-year contract in his pocket, Himes guaranteed results. He helped nudge the White Sox out of the doldrums by trading away South Side favorite Harold Baines in a deal that brought teenager Sosa to Chicago in midseason 1989, so he saw something in the erratic youngster that others didn't.

Ultimately, Himes was right about Sosa, wrong on his own ability to wheel and deal the Cubs into contention. At the end of Himes's three years, the Cubs had sandwiched one winning season between two losing ones, and he got kicked downstairs to a scouting post.

No Free Lynch for Cubs

The Sosa controversy evolved into a Sosa coronation when a blend of maturity, experience and hero worship from Cubs fans hungry for a superstar enabled this talented hombre to become The Man. Because Ed Lynch won't go down in history as the general manager who traded Sammy Sosa (although the final decision was not in his hands), he didn't go down himself until July 19, 2000. Lynch lasted five and a half years on the general manager's hot seat, longer than anyone except Dallas Green in the last quarter-century. The Cubs backed into the 1998 playoffs as the NL's wild card during his tenure, but without Sosa's gigantic presence, Lynch almost certainly would have been gone before then.

The job was too big for the former Mets and Cubs pitcher, a fact he affirmed by trying to quit even before the axe descended. Lynch was the first ex-Cub to run the front office since former first baseman Jolly Cholly Grimm, way back in the Wrigley era. He knew not to start sending out his laundry when the Cubs collapsed into the NL Central basement at 67-95 in 1999. Lynch had to run up the white flag of surrender with two months to go in that dismal season, although manager Jim Riggleman walked the plank first.

"We're looking at young people," Lynch admitted. "Mistakes will be made. All we can ask is for them to show up on time and play hard."

Sammy Handy for Andy

Sosa's sensational socking convinced Andy MacPhail to end the stay-or-go speculation by signing the superstar to a $72 million contract in full expectation that his career would end in Chicago. Slammin' Sammy hysteria overflowed Wrigley Field as his homer output soared from 33 in 1993 to 40 in '96 to 66 in '98—the year of the great fence-busting derby with Mark McGwire—to another brace of 60-plus seasons, to the threshold of joining Ernie Banks in the 500 club when he clubbed his first 2003 round-tripper.

Put Trust in Dusty

That wasn't enough, something Cubs president MacPhail acknowledged when he stepped into Lynch's job. Now Jim Hendry is the new rebuilding specialist for the Cubs, although MacPhail holds Tribune Co.'s purse strings. Shelling out $18 million for Dusty Baker to become shepherd of the Cubs flock led fans to believe that the Cubs will go on a spree in '03. Ernie Banks is sure to predict some such glad tidings this year, next year and every year, which is why his eternal optimism earned him the title of Mr. Cub. He wears it well. Some names fit snugly, like Wrigley Field's description—naturally, hung on it by Banks—the Friendly Confines.

Diz Knows How It Is

The great Dizzy Dean finished his career with the Cubs in 1941, unfortunately, after a liner by Earl Averill in the 1934 All-Star Game broke Diz's toe, altered his pitching motion and doused the flame in his fastball. But nothing could quench the irrepressible spirit of this homespun philosopher. His language manglings were as popular in their day as Harry Caray's "Lemme hear ya!"— for instance, "He slud into third" and "the runners are returning to their respectable bases." Dean also made a lot of sense, especially when he said, "I'd rather be lucky than good."

Where's Dame Fortune?

The Cubs have been neither for a long time. Their fans can be excused for believing the law of averages got repealed more than 50 years ago. Luck plays a major role on the diamond every season, another reason for the game's enduring popularity. Baseball is a lot like life, because the good guys don't always win, and teams that seemed destined for the playoffs get riddled by devastating injuries. That sort of bad luck bedeviled the Cubs in 2001, when Bill Mueller came from San Francisco to solve their perennial quandary—who's the next Ron Santo? As the 17th Cub to open the season at third base since Santo departed in 1974, Mueller was answering that question swiftly and efficiently, at the plate and around the hot corner.

Then, just 36 games into his sparkling debut, Mueller broke his left kneecap in St. Louis. Just like that, the Cubs were back to their annual game of Russian roulette, rushin' hot third-base prospects into the lineup and shipping them back to the bushes when they panned out so poorly that even those ever-patient Wrigley fans panned them. The total of would-be Cub third-sackers who got the sack since Santo's 1960-73 reign is close to 100. His mark of 2,102 games at that position seems safe for the rest of the century, if not forever.

Let's Not Make a Deal

"I've been offered a lot of trade possibilities," MacPhail said. "In my judgment, they would have been bad for the Cubs. We won't overlook any possible ways to improve the team."

For now, at least, the dream of a contending club rests with young talent in the farm system. The Cubs will go with them. The only question left for Cubs fans is obvious—in which direction?

1969—Fine Vine Wine or Sour Grapes?

Finally, it all comes back to that wonderful summer of 1969. For thousands—maybe millions—of Baby Boomers in Chicago and across the country, that was a defining moment in their lives. There was joy in Wrigley

Field, in stark contrast to the upheaval elsewhere in America. Then, in the last month, the prize got snatched away from the Cubs and their fans.

The unanswered questions raised then still hang over Wrigley Field, although not as severely as the hangovers at Murphy's Bleachers, the postgame hangout for True Believers in those days. Did the fold of '69 set the pattern for all the Cubs' failures since then? Or did it test the mettle of lifelong Cubs fans, making them even more determined to stick with this snake-bitten team through thin and thinner?

I honestly do not know. Of all the thousands of words written about that quixotic, crazy-quilt season, this parting reflection from Cubs owner P. K. Wrigley seems to sum it up best:

"It only takes a few minutes to go from a hero to a bum."

In the meantime, Cubs fans, just wait till next year.

Celebrate the Heroes of Chicago Sports and Baseball
in These Other Acclaimed Titles from Sports Publishing!